Wattle Hurdles
and
Leather Gaiters

Jacqueline A Z Ansch

1996

D1494676

Wattle Hurdles
and
Leather Gaiters

John Randall

FARMING PRESS

First published 1995

Copyright © 1995 John Randall

All rights reserved. No parts of this
publication may be reproduced, stored in
a retrieval system, or transmitted, in any
form or by any means, electronic, mechanical,
photocopying, recording or otherwise, without
prior permission of Farming Press Books & Videos.

ISBN 0 85236 306 0

A catalogue record for this book is available
from the British Library

Published by Farming Press Books
Miller Freeman Professional Ltd
Wharfedale Road, Ipswich IP1 4LG, United Kingdom

Distributed in North America
by Diamond Farm Enterprises,
Box 537, Alexandria Bay, NY 13607, USA

Front cover photograph by Andrew Shaylor
Cover design by Mark Beesley

Typeset by Galleon Typesetting, Ipswich
Printed and bound by Biddles Ltd,
Guildford and King's Lynn

Foreword

By the Lady Aldington

I fell under the spell of John Randall's story-telling one cold wet evening when several of us were sitting in the back of a lorry after showing sheep at the Kent County Show some twenty-five years ago. I remember wishing the evening would go on forever – this commanding man so enthralled us all.

Some time later when the Jacob Sheep Society was first given classes at several shows, we had no official judges of our own and were definitely sniffed at as being "little old ladies with their pet sheep spending their time weaving and spinning". It was suggested that I ask "Mr. Randall", as he was then known to me, if he would consider becoming our first judge. "If you get him, they will all stop laughing in a few years," Charlie Aves pronounced. I feel certain that behind the scenes this was the case, so when John asked me to write the foreword to his book I was delighted to be able to repay his kindness in agreeing to be our judge – even if he did consider that our sheep at the time were "pintle bottomed and goose arsed"!

It is rare to find a book so vivid in its pictures of everyday life on a farm that one can actually smell the wheelwright's shop, the hay making and the sausages frying in the make-shift kitchen in the back of a cattle wagon. The book is also full of highly amusing anecdotes. What is unique is that the writer is able to put on paper his own experiences from boyhood combined with such clear details concerning a good many of those crafts now lost "due to that Austrian Corporal", as he puts it, who was able to change the whole way of country life in just seven years.

I feel strongly that his vignette, a link between the past and the present day, should be read by all true countrymen. The author, still to be seen in his highly polished leather gaiters, is himself the epitome of the true country gentleman.

ARAMINTA ALDINGTON

Acknowledgements

My sincere thanks to

The late Charles Hammick, without whose help, encouragement and enthusiasm this book would never have been written

Paul Heiney, for his assistance in getting it published

Naomi Morrison, for reviewing the manuscript, and Jane Mayo and her sister Nicola, who typed the original copy

To Dorothy

Beckington

MY childhood and schooldays were spent in Beckington, a North Somerset village below the Mendip
Hills. The village, built around a major road junction, was
not the typical picture-postcard village of thatch and cob.
It had then, and still has to me, a certain hard austerity
about it, lacking the mellow warmth of West Dorset.

We were, I suppose, rather modern for the times; mains
electricity came in 1932. I well remember waiting for
the lights to come on for the first time one evening in
October. Mains water came in 1937, although many of
the older people still kept their own supply. My mother
used her pump until her death in the early 1970s. The
village was a very self-contained community with a doctor,
policeman, church, chapel, school, baker, grocer, butcher,
post office, blacksmith, wheelwright and a garage (which
also charged the accumulators for the wireless sets for six
old pence).

My father was the local wheelwright and carpenter and
the business had been in the family for many generations.
He was a great craftsman himself and very proud of the
family reputation. The workshop adjoined our home and
as a boy I spent a great deal of time watching carts and
wagons being made and repaired. Virtually all the timber
used was English hardwood, most of which was locally
grown. Father used to buy trees from the local estates and
have them planked out at the sawmills in a neighbouring
village, then brought home to be stacked for seasoning.

The time allowed was a year an inch: two-inch planks, two years; four-inch planks, four years. The workshop had a smell of its own – a mixture of sawdust, shavings and paint. Even the paint was made at home and consisted of red lead, white lead, ochre, linseed oil and turps.

The frames and undercarriages of the wagons were made of oak, the bottoms and sides of elm, shafts of ash, wheel boxes of either elm or apple and the spokes oak or felloes elm. With the exception of the wheels, the wagons were made from wooden templates, one for every piece of timber in the frame. The templates were kept and used time and time again; a separate set for each different size of wagon or cart. Making the wheels was an art in itself. The wheel box, or hub, was made first and was turned to shape and size on a pedal-operated lathe. The mortices for the spokes were then cut into it, generally twelve in all. Before the spokes were fitted, two metal rings, or bands, were sweated on each end of the box to stop it splitting. A tapered hole was then drilled through the centre of the hub with a tool known as a boxing engine. Into this was filled the tapered cast iron sleeve which fitted over the stub axle. The spokes were then fitted. The tenon which went into the box was rectangular and the tenon at the other end round. The curved felloes were then fitted onto the round end of the spokes – two spokes in each felloe. The felloes were then driven up tight onto the spokes and the wheel was ready for bonding. The outside of the wheel was measured with a metal wheel on a handle called a traveller. The iron tyre, or bond, was made a little smaller than the wheel. It was then heated until red hot, which allowed it to expand enough to be forced over the wheel. Water was then poured on to cool the bond and as it contracted it squeezed the wheel up tight.

My Uncle Charlie, who was the local blacksmith, was always in charge of the bonding and we used to watch the proceedings from a safe distance. Picking up a four-foot diameter, four-inch bond when it was red hot and placing it over the wheel demanded skill and strength. As soon as it was in place and the water was applied the complete operation was blanketed in steam and smoke and, as often happened if someone got a boot full of water in the process, a stream of bad language.

One of the great attractions of the blacksmith's shop was Bill Millett, a genial character known to everyone as Tiger, who worked for Uncle Charlie. He was a sparsely built man in his late forties with a luxuriant moustache, steel-rimmed glasses and clay pipe. His pipe, with a stem no more than three inches long, seemed never to leave his mouth and appeared to be embedded in his moustache, which always looked to be in immediate danger of catching fire, especially when he lit up. Tiger, an old soldier, had served in the Army as a farrier. He had a great vocabulary, much of which was unprintable. He was also a great story teller, mainly about his service in India just before the First World War. As boys we used to love to be allowed to blow the bellows for him when he was shoe making or shoeing. He was the fastest and one of the finest shoeing smiths I have ever met.

At that time all the farms in the district were still using horses and most of Tiger's time was taken up either with shoeing or making shoes for heavy horses. I can picture him now in his leather apron, his pipe going full blast with the smoke coming out of his moustache as he picked up a cart horse's foot with his customary "Hist up, ut." Slipping the foot between his legs and gripping it there he could apply the new shoes heated red hot and held with a punch driven into one of the nail holes until it had burnt into the horn of the foot to become a perfect fit. He would be lost in a cloud of smoke as this took place. After fitting all four shoes he then nailed them into place at great speed with seven nails known as hoss studs. Sometimes when shoeing colts or horses with itchy legs they kicked out and Tiger would be flung across the yard. On these occasions the air was blue and as the blacksmith's shop was in the centre of the village, a lot of people would hear it. On one occasion the vicar took Tiger to task over his language and said that *he* was very often upset but never had to resort to bad language. "You bloody well would if you had been kicked half way across the yard by that itchy legged great sod," retorted Tiger.

Another favourite was old Jim Wheeler, a grand old gentleman in his late sixties, who worked for father as a wheelwright. He had been apprenticed to my grandfather and worked for the family all his life. He lived on his own, having never married, and was a fount of knowledge on country matters and customs, as well as being quite a herbalist. Every summer he used to collect many plants, including half a dozen or so big puff balls, which were then placed on a shelf in the workshop. After several months they had dried out – the outside skin became tough as leather and the centre was reduced to a brown powder. This powder was saved and put into a tin, then used on any cuts as a wound dressing. It was very effective in stopping bleeding and the cuts always seemed to heal without any infection. The powder was, after all, derived from a fungus. Could it perhaps have been a crude type of penicillin? One of my aunts was a Nursing Sister in Queen Alexandra's Royal Army Nursing Service and used to spend her holidays with us. I well remember how she used to carry on if she caught anyone using Jim's powder, but the stuff worked and in spite of her objections it was used frequently.

Our village policeman was a man who would have been a cartoonist's dream – six feet tall and about fifteen stone with a name to fit – PC Billy Button. He had an air of solid dignity whether on duty or umpiring the village cricket matches and was always the same, quite unflappable. Apart from the odd bit of poaching, crime locally seemed to be non-existent and rarely did he have to summons anyone. He had his ear to the ground, however, and very little, if anything, went on in the village without his knowledge. As a boy, if you met him walking down the street you politely wished him good day and hoped that he had not heard of any mischief that he could connect with you. If he had, you would be most likely to get a good ticking off and a cuff around the ears for good measure and if you protested your innocence you were sure to get a second.

On one never-to-be-forgotten occasion the gipsies from Stowe Fair camped in an old green lane outside the village for a few days. On a Saturday morning they were at the local pub making a nuisance of themselves. A group of village boys was watching the fun from the opposite side of the road. Things were getting out of hand and the landlady sent her son to fetch the policeman. Bill Button came up the road on his bicycle (he had a habit of cycling slower than he walked). When he reached the pub he dismounted and, totally ignoring the noise from inside where all hell seemed to have broken loose, he bent down and removed his cycle clips, straightened his tunic and helmet, squared his shoulders and marched in. The noise suddenly subsided and then, like corks from a champagne bottle, the gipsies came flying out the door to finish up in a heap in the middle of the road. PC Button stood in the doorway for a minute or two, then said: "Now then, you lot, get back to your vans, sober up, hitch up and get the hell out of here by the morning." With that he disappeared back into the pub. The gipsies picked themselves up, got into their pony traps and drove off. Curious as boys always are, we wondered what was going on inside, so crept to the window and peeped in. Billy Button was sitting at the bar in his shirt sleeves, a pint pot in his hand, having a well-deserved drink. His tunic was neatly folded on the bar beside him with his helmet on top. He was off duty.

On his retirement from the police force several years later he became the landlord of the Foresters Arms which he ran very successfully for the rest of his life. He was, I suppose, the typical country policeman of the times. He knew everyone on his beat and if there was any trouble he knew exactly where to go and who to go to, in most cases stamping on it before it got out of hand. Years later, when he was referred to as a real gentleman in the presence of Silas, one of the local poachers, old Silas replied: "He were real and he were a man right enough but I bain't so sure about the gentle bit."

The village school was a typical Victorian building constructed of local stone with a tile roof. It consisted of a long, narrow room divided into three by two wooden and glass partitions which could be removed, turning the school into a village hall for functions such as concerts, dances and whist drives. These events always had to take place either at weekends or during the school holidays. There was a smaller range of buildings at right angles to the main school. These housed the cloakrooms and toilets and formed two sides of the tarmac playground. Central heating had been installed in the early 1920s and electricity in the mid-thirties. Without a playing field, inside toilets, hot water or a gymnasium, it would be totally unacceptable today but no one seemed to suffer for it and we were given an excellent grounding in reading, writing and arithmetic.

There were three teachers including the headmistress who, like the village policeman, knew about any mischief going on both in and out of school but, unlike Billy Button, she had a different way of dealing with it, rarely resorting to corporal punishment. She could, and would, reduce anyone to tears with her biting sarcasm. The one thing she insisted on at all times and from everyone was courtesy and good manners. One of her favourite sayings was "Civility costs you nothing." Thinking back to those days I am convinced that her quiet, firm discipline and insistence on courtesy to everyone no matter who, was a wonderful way to start learning about life.

We had the usual village organisations: Scouts, Guides, WI, etc., a rather mediocre football team and a very good cricket team. Our cricket pitch was on the recreation field complete with cricket hut and pavilion. Father was still playing, although getting on a bit. He was quite a useful bat and a good slow bowler, tossing them up very much like the old Somerset captain, Farmer White. My brother, Stewart, was also a regular member of the team. In the last couple of seasons before the war he developed into a really good fast bowler. I had graduated from scorer to twelfth man and was getting the odd game whenever someone had to drop out. Cricket was very much a family sport.

A line of tall elm trees used to start at the top end of the cricket field and no matter what the state of the game Father was always put on to bowl at that end just as the sun dipped below the tree tops. In that light he was virtually unplayable and generally took several quick wickets. This used to lead to complaints from the visiting team. These were always settled by our umpire, Bill Button, retorting: "I know you loses sight of the ball against the trees but it's as bad for the keeper as it is for you." He had an air of finality about him which brooked no argument. He umpired with the dignity that was his hallmark. On confirming an appeal his right hand, with index finger extended, would rise in the same slow, stately manner. Denying an appeal, especially if it was frivolous, involved a look of disgusted amazement. On one occasion the visiting team's last man was in and not getting on very well. On the last ball of the over he was rapped on the pads and the bowler appealed for LBW, more in hope than expectation, but instead of getting the usual amazed look from Bill, his hand made its stately ascent. As they all walked back to the pavilion the batsman caught up with Bill and told him that he did not consider that he had been standing in front of the wicket. "I know you were not, son," came the reply, "but the ladies have had the tea ready for the last ten minutes."

Tea was always provided by the home team and grand ones they were. There were trestle tables laid out either in front of the pavilion or inside according to the weather, and they were laden with sandwiches and home-made cakes prepared by the wives of the home team. Indeed, some of the villages were more renowned for their teas than their cricket.

Another local character was Peggy Attfield, a hard-as-nails countryman who had lost his right leg on the Somme. He had a wooden peg leg from the knee down, hence his nickname, but he never let this disability get in the way of either work or pleasure. For many years he drove a timber hauling outfit, transporting tree trunks, or butts as they were called, from the farms and woodlands to the local sawmills. His outfit consisted of a Fowler steam traction engine fitted with a timber winch which pulled a timber carriage.

These timber carriages were specially made for the job and at that time most were constructed completely of wood. They consisted of two pairs of wheels, each mounted on a very strong axle. The front pair were made to swivel or lock so the carriage could be manoeuvred into awkward places and were connected to the traction engine with a massive draw bar. The two axles were connected by means of a long pole, one end of which was fixed to the front axle and the other end slid through the back axle with a large metal pin through both pole and axle to hold it in place. The idea was that when hauling short butts the back wheels could be slid up the pole, thereby shortening the length of the carriage; they were then slid back for longer butts, thus distributing the weight equally on all wheels. The tops of the axles were built up with baulks of timber until they were over the top of the wheels and onto these were loaded the tree trunks. A strong piece of timber was placed from the top of each axle to the ground, forming a ramp, up which the tree trunks were rolled using the winch of the traction engine.

Construction of these wheels was similar to that of wagon wheels, but they were much stronger and only about three feet to three feet six inches in diameter. They had massive boxes, very short, strong spokes and five- or six-inch felloes and bonds. Like wagon wheels they had a cast iron sleeve fitted through the centre of the box into which the metal axle fitted. If for any reason these sleeves were loose in the wheel box and failed to turn with the wheel, they would quickly wear away the wood around them. If this was not spotted quickly the wheel would collapse. This trouble was more prevalent in timber carriage wheels because of the extra weight they carried compared to a wagon. When it happened, the wheels had to be taken off, the metal sleeves removed and realigned in the centre hole and then fixed firmly with a series of wooden wedges overlapping each other. Great care had to be taken that the metal sleeve was fixed dead centre or else the wheel would wobble. The wedges had to be driven home very tight or the sleeve would fail to turn with the wheel. This process was known as "boxing a wheel" and was one of the many arts of the wheelwright.

I had just returned home from school one summer afternoon and was in the shop where Father and Jim Wheeler were working on a wagon when Peggy came tap tapping with his wooden leg into the shop.

"Yer Dick, I be in trouble. Wants a bit of help, quick like," he said.

"What is the matter?" Father enquired.

"Me near-side back carriage wheel wants boxing bad, cans't do it straight away?"

"All right," Father replied. "Bring her up outside and we'll do it there right."

"Can't do that, Dick. Got three girt elm butts on and she be wobbling like hell. 'Fraid to move her any further. I got her pulled in on Woolpack yard."

Father scratched his head and looked worried. "Look Peggy, we can box the wheel no trouble but I ain't got anything strong enough to lift a loaded carriage."

Peggy grinned all over his face. "That's all right, Dick, thee just bring on thee tackle. I can get her up simple like."

Father and Jim picked up their tools and a supply of wedges which were always kept cut out for such jobs. We walked down the street some three hundred yards to the Woolpack yard just off the road. The steam engine and timber carriage were pulled in, loaded with three massive tree trunks, the back near-side wheel leaning at a drunken angle. Jim Wheeler walked round and inspected the damaged wheel.

"By God, Peggy, thee's reamered half the box away; been giving her a main bit of stick hassen?"

"How the hell's think I got her up over Clifford Hill with a load like that on if I didn't?" came the reply. Peggy called to his mate who also acted as steersman: "Fred, let's have the pinch bar and the jacking stump."

Fred fetched the iron pinch bar and Peggy proceeded to pick out a small hole, a foot square and six to eight inches deep in the stone surfaced yard, about two feet in front of the back axle and close up to the damaged wheel. Fred had by then brought out the jacking stump. This was a stout piece of oak, six inches in diameter and about three feet long with a fork at one end like a giant catapult stick. Then Peggy outlined his plan and gave his orders.

"I going to get down under carriage, stick stump in this hole and hold fork up to the axle. Fred, when I shouts, you eases engine up real steady like and when I hollers 'Whoa', you stops sharpish mind. You two", addressing Father and Jim, "you chocks up the wheel as soon as she stops." (Peggy had not been a Sergeant for nothing.)

Father protested, "Don't be such a bloody fool Peggy. You reckon you going to lie under carriage, holding that stump up to the axle while Fred moves her up? Supposing she goes too far or she slides sideways? That wheel won't stand the jar when she comes down and you would be squatted flat as a turd."

"What be grumbling about?" came the reply. "If that happens thees have a wheel to box and a box to make as well." (Father was the local undertaker.) "But bless ee, that won't happen. Now stop mithering and let's get on with it."

Peggy lay on his back and wriggled under the carriage, bumped the butt end of the stump into the hole he had dug out and held the fork up under the axle, the stump leaning at about a forty-five degree angle. On the word of command, Fred very slowly eased the steam engine forward, the fork slipped under the axle and, as the carriage moved forward, the damaged wheel slowly came clear of the ground. The instant the stump became upright Peggy's yell brought the engine to a stop and Father and Jim chocked up the off-side wheel. Peggy crawled out, hopped up and proceeded to dust himself down.

"She be all yours, Dick. Told thee there was nothing to it. Hi, Fred," he shouted to his mate. "Get in Woolpack and bring out four pints."

11

"'Tis only a quarter to six," came the reply.

"Get round the back door, you bloody fool," roared Peggy. Turning back to Father and Jim he shook his head. "That feller be terrible thick at times," he grumbled.

Father and Jim took out the lynchpin that held the wheel in place, removed it and got to work on the box which was badly reamered out. After about an hour the job was done to their mutual satisfaction. The wheel was replaced, the carriage gently eased back off the stump and with a blast of the whistle Peggy moved off to deliver his load.

The school was sometimes used for private parties. On one occasion a family who had moved into one of the large houses in the village several years previously hired it for their daughter's twenty-first birthday party. Reasonably wealthy, with an urban background, they had always considered themselves rather superior and refrained from taking part in any local activity. In village language they were "a right toffee-nosed lot".

Father had been engaged to take down the partitions in the school and haul the chairs and tables required. The village owned quite a number of these which were kept in the Rectory stables and could be hired for a nominal fee. The partitions were taken down and all the school desks removed to the cloakrooms first thing in the morning. The chairs and tables were taken up in the afternoon, by which time the school had been decorated and a firm of caterers had arrived. As the chairs were being unloaded the lady of the house informed Father that a band had been engaged for dancing but she did not consider the school piano was of a sufficient standard and would he fetch their baby grand to take its place. This was done after a struggle; getting a piano onto and off a wagonette takes a bit of doing. Then Father drove off home leaving several of us to put the chairs and tables in place. We were rather

12

disgruntled with the whole job, especially Fred Webly, who played the piano in the village dance band. The caterers had disappeared but had left all the food and drink locked in their van.

"This is a damn bright do," grumbled Fred. "Been lugging chairs all afternoon, then this ugly girt piano and now they been and locked all the grub up. Been old Bill Valentine (the local baker) doing it, we'd have had a right skinful. Me band ain't good enough for 'em and now the old piano ain't wanted. Yer wonder what their box of tricks sounds like." He sat down and played for a while; he was quite a good pianist. Then a grin slowly spread over his face. "Tell ee what, chaps, let's tune the damn thing." Off came the top, out came a pair of pliers and Fred proceeded to tune, slackening a wire here and tightening another there.

On returning the piano the next day we were told that it had been impossible to use as the move had upset the tuning. Father smelled a rat straight away. "What you young devils been up to?" he demanded. "You got messing about with that piano when my back was turned. It was all right when I ran my hand over it last night before I left."

We all assumed an air of injured innocence. "How could we do that governor?" asked Fred. "We ain't got no tuning key."

"No, but you had a pair of pliers," snapped Father. His eyes lighting up, he opened the piano and scrutinised all the tuning pins for scratch marks but could find none. Fred had done the job properly, wrapping each pin he moved with his handkerchief before gripping it with the pliers. Father ran his fingers over the keys and found the ones that were out of tune. Again he scrutinised the pins. "How the hell did you manage that?" he grunted.

"Well, it's like you always telling us," replied Fred. "If a job is worth doing it's worth doing well."

Father was a well-known and respected pillar of village life. Born in the old family home in Goose Street, he lived there until his marriage. He then moved next door and spent the rest of his life there. He took a great interest in the well-being of the village, serving on most of its bodies: he was Clerk to the Parish Council for forty years, retiring to become its Chairman; he represented the village on the Rural District Council for over twenty years; and he was Churchwarden and on the Board of Governors of Frome Grammar School. His other great pride was his work. In this he was a perfectionist and very conservative. I remember a local farmer ordering a new two-horse wagon from him. They had agreed the price but the farmer wanted it painted red and blue. Father replied that for over a hundred years Randall's wagons had always been finished yellow and red and he was not prepared to change. He got the order on his terms. He used to tell us boys that success in life was like success at cards. It did not consist of being dealt a good hand but of playing a bad hand well.

Following in Mother's Footsteps

MOTHER was a proud, outspoken countrywoman. She came from a family who had made Cheddar cheese on the Mendips and Somerset Levels for over a hundred years, the art of cheese making having been passed from mother to daughter for generations. She was one of three sisters, all of whom were cheese makers of repute and consistent prizewinners at the Agricultural Shows of the time. She came to the village in 1910 to make cheese at one of the larger dairy farms. Her salary of twenty-six pounds per annum with all found made her the highest paid member of the farm staff. The head dairyman received fourteen shillings per week, on which he had to keep himself, his wife and family. Mother used to tell us that at the time she was able to save at least fifteen pounds a year out of her salary, which was paid twice yearly on Lady Day, March 25th, and Michaelmas, September 29th. She also received half the prize money won by cheeses she had made.

Mother never lost her love of animals and her interest in farming. She always kept hens and, up to the 1950s, a pig or two. We had a smart, fast bay cob until the late thirties, which Mother used to drive with quite a dash. She bought a black mare with her own money when she married Father and used to boast that it could trot on the level between two milestones in three minutes. Farmer Veisey, who had known her family for years, maintained that she was as good as her mother with horses: they could both drive through the eye of a needle.

Her sister, Rose, and husband, Bert, were farming in West Dorset and we used to go there for a few days at Whitsun and August Bank Holiday. Mother used to insist on making the cheese while we were there, her excuse being that it gave Aunt Rose a break. I am sure the real reason was to show everyone that the old skill was still there, for on several occasions the cheese she made went on to be a prizewinner. She was just that little better at the job than Aunt Rose and I am sure that she knew it. She had two favourite sayings which I have always thought summed up her character:

"Right's right and wrong is no man's right."

"Tis better to live in spite than in pity."

In the early thirties Father had his first motor car, a two-seater bull-nosed Morris Cowley tourer with a dicky seat in the back. She had three forward gears and reverse, back wheel brakes only, a horn that you had to squeeze, hand-operated windscreen wipers, no door on the driver's side, a canvas hood and she was fitted with a French-made engine. Being rather low geared she went uphill like smoke. When passing other cars, especially on an incline, they were given a cheer and a wave from two small boys in the dicky seat. We used to think she was wonderful. It was quite an adventure to travel the fifty miles from home to West Dorset, a journey of about one-and-three-quarter hours. Incidentally, Shell Mex petrol was then one shilling and four pence a gallon.

From the age of ten I started to spend my school holidays with Aunt Rose and Uncle Bert at Limbury, their farm in West Dorset, and what a wonderful place it was for a boy before the days of mechanisation and specialisation. The farm was situated about half a mile from a small village. It was a large, rambling eighteenth-century farmhouse complete with dairy and cheese room. On one end was the stable yard and beyond that the cattle yard with cowsheds forming two sides, pig sties the third side and a large pond at the front which provided water for the animals.

The main enterprise was a dairy herd of great, deep-bodied, placid, red, roan and white Shorthorn cows with their lovely, curved-in horns. In the summer holidays I used to have to help fetch them in for milking. After a few calls they would slowly get up and make a leisurely start for the gate. You walked around behind them to keep them moving, as they stopped here and there to tear off a mouthful of grass, swishing their tails and occasionally swinging their heads to dislodge the flies. The cow shed had a crib, or manger, along the front wall in which fodder could be placed. Round posts about four inches in diameter were set in the crib four feet apart. An iron ring with cow chain attached was loosely fitted to each post. Each chain had three round links at one end and a T-piece at the other. The chain was put around the cow's neck, the T-piece slipped through the round link and she was tied up. Cows are very much creatures of habit and would always go into the same place in the shed. It was very difficult to get them to change places if for any reason you wanted to move them around. By the thirties most sheds had concrete floors and gutters which were much easier to keep clean than the older cobblestone or brick ones.

The dairy at Limbury was a long, lean-to room built on the back and extending half the length of the farmhouse. Two windows looked out over the orchard. There were two doors, one opening directly into the farm kitchen and the other onto the cobbled back yard which contained the lead-barrelled pump and its stone pump trough, the only water supply for the house and dairy.

With its unplastered whitewashed walls, blue flagstone floor and a large copper in the far corner for heating water, the dairy had an almost clinical atmosphere about it. A large copper cheese tub with a brass tap stood in the centre of the room with three cheese presses, two double and one single, along the back wall. A curd tub stood next to the copper. One's first impression was of utter cleanliness. The floor was scrubbed as smooth as marble and all the equipment shone like a silver sixpence.

The actual cheese making used to take up to eight hours every day. Just after six o'clock, Aunt Rose would fill the copper with water from the pump in the courtyard and light up so that there was plenty of hot water to wash the milking buckets and heat the milk when milking finished just after seven. The process for heating the milk, and later the whey, was to put about six to eight gallons in what was called a cooler – a ten-gallon container with handles on both sides. This was lifted into the copper of hot water and allowed to heat up, then placed in the cheese tub.

When all the day's milk was in the tub, the temperature was raised to 90°F and the starter and rennet added. The tub was covered with a blanket for about an hour, by which time the milk, under the influence of the rennet, had turned into junket. This was then cut into pieces about the size of an Oxo cube with a curd knife, a metal frame about two feet six inches long by nine inches wide set with blades every inch. Known as curd, this was the solid content of the milk which would eventually become cheese. The liquid, which accounted for up to four-fifths of the milk, had by now turned to whey, in which the curds floated. At this stage the mixture was again heated and some of the whey was drawn off, warmed in the copper and returned to the tub. A curd breaker was used to stir the mixture of curds and whey and, when heated, the pieces of curd gradually reduced in size as the whey was expelled from them until they were about the size of a pea.

It took about one-and-a-half hours from the time the junket was cut until the curd was allowed to drop. This timing was determined by testing the whey with an acidity meter. Aunt Rose always seemed to use her instinct in this. She would feel, smell and taste a piece of curd and, when satisfied, would then test it to confirm that she was right. After the curd had been stirred, it dropped to the bottom of the tub where it formed a thick layer. It was allowed to remain for about another hour.

The whey was then drawn off, leaving the curds on the bottom of the tub. By this time they had solidified enough to be cut into lumps about as big as bricks and removed to the curd tub where they were covered with a blanket and a weight to expel as much whey as possible. The slabs of curd were then turned over every half hour or so. All this time a small amount of whey kept seeping out. This was tested and when the right acidity had been reached the curd was put through the curd mill (a large mincing machine), salt was added and then the curd was packed into cheese moulds and pressed for three days. Aunt Rose used to make fourteen-pound truckles. After pressing, these were greased with lard and sewn up in butter muslin bandages. The cheeses were stored on shelves in the cheese room where they were turned over every day and allowed to mature for about six months before sale.

This must seem rather a primitive way of cheese making, but the result was a mild cheese with a slightly crumbly texture that left a tang in the mouth – so different from the modern, tasteless, rubbery-textured, vacuum-packed, unmatured product one so often finds on super-market shelves. Looking back, the thing that still amazes me was how the farm wives of that period ever managed to run a house, raise a family and make cheese at the same time, bearing in mind that they had no running water, electricity or gas.

Nothing was wasted in those days; the whey was used to fatten pigs. Uncle Bert always maintained that the profit derived from making cheese as opposed to selling the milk was not enough to justify the extra work, but linking it with fattening pigs made the enterprise worthwhile. Pig keeping was so different then. There were none of the present day specialised units of hundreds of sows, but nearly every farm had a few pigs running about and, in most cases, fattened all the piglets. How Uncle Bert managed his pigs was typical of the area and times. Saddleback sows were always used. They were mated to a Large White boar to produce a long, blue and white pig which at the time was very popular with the bacon curers and butchers. Most years a single sow would be bred pure to produce gilts to maintain the herd. In those days one never bought anything that one could produce oneself.

From the time the piglets were weaned until they were due to farrow, the sows ran about in an old orchard which had a thatched shed in the corner where they used to lie, well bedded up with straw. When they were close to farrowing they were moved into loose boxes which had rails fixed around them about nine inches off the floor and offset the same distance from the walls. This enabled the sows to lie down without the risk of them lying on the baby piglets. The piglets were weaned at eight weeks and allowed to run in a large yard for a couple of months before being put into the fattening houses. Each house contained ten to twelve pigs. At that time, pigs were taken to much greater weights, eight to ten score (160–200 pounds) dressed carcase weight being quite common.

The fattening pigs were fed entirely on a mixture of whey and barley meal. The meal store was situated on the end of the fattening house. Two large tubs were used to hold the whey; the barley meal was added until the mixture reached the consistency of thin porridge. It was then dipped out in old milking buckets and poured into the pig troughs through pipes in the walls. The moment you entered the meal house and started to mix up all hell was let loose. With forty or fifty pigs screaming their heads off, it was impossible to hear yourself speak. As soon as the food was in the troughs the noise ceased abruptly, the silence broken only by an occasional grunt.

I well remember Uncle Bert having an argument with his brother-in-law who maintained that selling milk paid better than making cheese. The old boy's reply was sharp and to the point: "With Russian barley at four pounds a ton and pigs at twelve and six a score, I make more out of the whey than you do out of the bloody milk."

On my first holiday in Dorset I learned how to hand milk. I was given a three-gallon tapered steel milking pail and a three-legged milking stool and sat down on the off-side (cows were only milked from one side) under a very quiet old cow named Strawberry. She was a large roan Shorthorn with tiny horns and a very placid nature. After being shown what to do I was left to it, with my head pressed into her flank. I squeezed away and after a minute or two the knack started to come and the bottom of the pail began to get covered with milk. Suddenly I felt warm, wet breath on the side of my face and a great, rough tongue rasped across my ear. I stared up right into her face; she looked at me with her great, doleful eyes as much as to say, "What the hell do you think you are doing?" Cows varied. Some you had to squeeze much harder to expel the milk, thus the term "hard milkers". Another disadvantage was teat size. Cows with over-large teats, known as bottle teats, were difficult to milk, especially if they were too big to get your hand right round, but the worst were the very short teats, especially on heifers. You had to strip them out finger and thumb, which took a long time.

I milked old Strawberry twice a day during that summer holiday, for about a fortnight. Uncle used to check to see if I had milked her out properly. I was a very proud boy one morning when he announced he would not bother to check again. By the end of the holiday I could make the pail ring with jets of milk when starting and get froth on the top of the milk like the head on a glass of beer – two of the important things that went towards making a good milker. An average milker could get through about eight cows an hour, a good one from ten to twelve. Although I say it myself, by the time I left school I was a good milker.

Aunt Rose, like a lot of the farmers' wives, looked after the poultry and the eggs provided her with pocket money. She used to keep about one hundred hens and hatch out about another hundred chicks each year. The pullets were kept for replacements and the cockerels were fattened for sale as table birds. Unlike Mother, who for years kept pure White Leghorns, she had a very mixed-up lot. Each year she would buy three or four cocks of the same breed, which were used for one year only, and then she would buy another bunch of a different breed. Over the years there were Rhode Island Reds, Light Sussex, Plymouth Rock, Buff Rocks, Marans and Indian Game. The result was hens all colours of the rainbow. Mother once described them as like a bag of liquorice allsorts without the liquorice.

The hens were kept in two large sheds at the bottom of the stable yard. They had the run of the farmyard and the buildings and were fed entirely on grain. The chickens were reared in a small orchard at the back of the dairy where they were reasonably safe from crows and magpies. One of my first jobs was to collect the eggs and look for stray nests. Some hens seemed to take a great delight in laying in the most inaccessible and unlikely places – in the back of cart sheds, in the horses' mangers, the cow cribs and around the hay and straw ricks. Some nests were never found and one morning the old hen would proudly lead out a dozen or so day-old chicks. Another of my early jobs was to pen up in the evenings. The hens generally went in without any trouble just before dark, but some of the young pullets and cockerels used to roost in the apple trees. It was great fun poking them out using a long ash pole with a fork at the top. You placed it under the branch they were roosting on, gave a good shake and, with a bit of luck, down they came. If any were left out, the chances were that a fox would have them by morning.

In the summer holidays the dairy herd was in full production. Hay making was finished by then and harvest just started – a harvest so different from today, with no combines, tractors and balers roaring round the fields but the creak of harness and the clink of chains as a three-horse team pulled a binder around the standing corn. The binder fans swished as they swept the corn onto the platform and the rattle of the canvas conveyors was punctuated every second or two by a thump as the knotter needle came round and tied each sheaf and kicked them out in neat rows ready for stooking. This consisted of taking a sheaf in each hand, driving the butts into the ground about two feet apart and bringing the tops together. Eight or ten sheaves formed a stook. After stooking, the crop was allowed to stand in the field to dry out before being put into ricks. Wheat and barley dried out quite quickly, in just a few days; oats took longer. According to custom they had to stand three Sundays in stook, in other words, at least a fortnight.

When hauling, a gang consisted of seven men, three wagons and four horses. Whilst one horse and wagon was being loaded in the field by two pitchers and one loader, one more was being unloaded in the rick yard with one man pitching off the sheaves and two more making the rick. The other horse and wagon, with an extra string harness horse, was employed with a carter hauling the loaded wagon from the field to the rick yard and the empty wagons back to the field. By so doing, everyone was kept continuously employed. For the first couple of harvests I used to lead the horse and wagon as it was being loaded, making sure to shout "Hold hard" to the loader before moving on to the next stook, and also taking great care not to let the wagon wheel go over a sheaf. This was considered almost a crime.

When I was fourteen I was promoted to driving loads: two horses at length with a loaded wagon. You walked by the head of the breeching horse with your right hand on its bridle and drove the front, or string harness horse with your left. With a "Stand up there", you were off, making for the field gate into the lane. The load was about seven feet wide, the gateway ten. Through you went, keeping as close to the off-side post as possible and driving the string harness horse right across the lane before allowing him to swing back left-handed, then keeping the breeching horse straight out into the lane before letting him follow round. If you let the horses turn too quickly you caught the gate post with the wheel. If this happened something generally got broken – either the gate post, the wagon shafts or the harness and then there would be hell to pay. Uncle, like most farmers, was always a bit short during hay making and harvest and any breakdown or hold-up used to get him on the rampage. After negotiating the gateway, the load was taken up the lane and into the rick yard where it was pulled alongside the elevator. The string harness horse was then hitched off, tied onto the back of the empty wagon and back you went to the field for another load. Just after tea, on my first day of driving loads, the field gang gave me a message for the rick maker that there were only three loads left. On returning with the next load I delivered my message to old Frank Parker, who replied very solemnly: "Right oh, Carter." At that moment I thought I was the cat's whiskers.

After the fields were cleared of sheaves they were horse raked. These rakings were always put in a rick on their own and when threshed out were used as chicken corn. There were very few Dutch barns about in those days and no plastic sheeting. The hay and corn ricks were thatched with wheat straw, which was pegged on with spars made from split hazel and willow. Farms, like villages, were pretty well self-contained: you bought as little as possible and wasted nothing.

By the time the Christmas holiday came around things had altered dramatically, for the dairy herd was spring calving. The cows were now nearly all dry or drying off and instead of spending their time out in the fields grazing, they were tied up in the cow sheds being fed hay and let out twice a day to drink while the sheds were cleaned out. The hay was all loose then and had to be cut out of the ricks in large slabs with a hay knife and carried into the cow sheds. It was not a very pleasant job in the rain and even worse in a gale-force wind.

Christmas is always a great occasion, but the Christmases of my boyhood stand out in my memory; so many things that we now have all the year round were then only annual luxuries. Our Christmases were very much family affairs.

Father had lost his parents at an early age – his mother when he was only nine and his father when he was twenty-one – so that we only knew one pair of grandparents, Grandmother and Grandfather Baker. On the surface they were typical Victorians. Grandfather was a very quiet, reserved gentleman with a neatly trimmed grey beard, who always wore a starched collar and tie and never seemed to get excited or angry. He was a monumental mason by trade and had spent most of his life on the restoration and maintenance of cathedrals and church structures. Grandmother was a tall, stately woman with a rather domineering character. She came from an old-established farming family and was the eldest daughter in a family of two boys and three girls. Her father had died when she was in her early twenties, her elder brother had taken over the farm and her mother had moved to a smaller farm with her younger son and three daughters.

Shortly after her father's death, Grandmother married and she and Grandfather bought a house adjoining the farm, where he set up his workshop. During the next ten years they produced a family of six, two boys and four girls, of whom Mother was the youngest. By this time Grandmother's younger brother had married and taken over the local mill which also had a small farm attached to it, leaving his mother running the home farm with two daughters still at home. When they in turn married, Grandmother went back to cheese making for her mother and, during the 1890s, took over the tenancy of the farm herself and continued to farm it for the next thirty years. Grandfather never had anything to do with the farm, continuing with his own profession until they both retired when in their seventies. This is why I say that they were typical Victorians on the surface only, for surely not many married couples of that period pursued their own separate careers after marriage, and very few ladies farmed in their own right. We always spent Christmas with them and as we were their only grandchildren we were shamefully spoilt.

We would arrive on the afternoon of Christmas Eve and be allowed to help put up the holly and paper chain decorations before tea, after which there was the tree to be decorated. This was always done under Grandmother's direction and watchful eye; she made sure that no chocolates or sugar mice were purloined or hidden away for secret consumption later. A rather battered angel was always fixed onto the top of the tree, which was draped in tinsel, then chocolate Father Christmases and little nets of foil-covered chocolate money and sugar mice were tied on. Next came the candles: little metal candle holders were clipped onto the branches and coloured candles inserted. At about half past seven we were packed off to bed with the promise that, if we behaved, we would be allowed to stay up for the party on Christmas night – not that there was any need to resort to bribery, for neither of us ever wanted to get on the wrong side of Grandmother. Playing up to Mother was one thing, playing up to Grandmother was quite a different matter. When she snapped at you in the same tone of voice she used on a recalcitrant cow or horse you moved sharply.

Christmas morning came and the stocking hung up the night before was full of oranges, nuts, sweets, a small toy or two and a little book; a pillow case held the bigger presents which we were not supposed to open until after breakfast, but curiosity invariably got the better of us and the corners were opened and carefully done up again. We might not have known exactly what each parcel contained but we had a good idea of what was inside. Breakfast (always boiled eggs) was dispatched at record speed and then the parcels were opened. They had to be unwrapped carefully and the brown wrapping paper saved for future use. At about eleven o'clock Father would take Grandfather, my brother and myself the couple of miles to spend an hour with Mother's brother, Ern, who farmed on the other side of the village. By the time we arrived Uncle would have finished work for the morning and the three men sat down with a bottle of Scotch; we were allowed the luxury of a glass of hot milk with a small nip of whisky added.

From an early age I realised that there was something different and special about Uncle Ern and as I got older I began to appreciate what it was. Standing six feet tall, slim and as upright as a ramrod, he walked with the unmistakable bearing of a soldier, having served for over twenty years in the Yeomanry. As a seventeen-year-old trooper he had fought in South Africa and August 1914 found him in France, by then a Squadron Sergeant Major. In the retreat from Mons he was awarded the Distinguished Conduct Medal and two years later, on the Somme, he gained the Bar to his DCM and was promoted to Regimental Sergeant Major. He used to tell us wonderful tales about South Africa, describing the country – trees, plants, animals and the people in great detail – but he never spoke of the war. Not until I was a young man did I hear him mention France.

I well remember him tearing a strip off father in 1938. Neville Chamberlain had just returned from Munich with the "Peace in our time" agreement. As we often did on a Sunday afternoon, Father had taken us to visit Uncle Ern and over tea the conversation came round to Chamberlain. Father, a lifelong dyed-in-the-wool Tory, thought he had done a good job and said so. "A good job be damned, Dick," snapped Uncle. "Have you ever knowed giving into anybody or anything work yet? If you got a chap working for you who is light fingered you got to stop him or he will keep at it; if he is lazy and you don't wake him up he won't alter; if you got a horse that runs away he got to be stopped or he will keep doing it. The same goes for a jibber (a carthorse that refuses to pull) and the same goes for Hitler; if he ain't stopped he will go on taking what he wants until they politicians finally find guts enough to stand up to him, then it's the army that's going to have to get 'em out of a mess yet again. The only things that saved us in 1914 was the Lee Enfield rifle and the standard of

28

musketry of the British Army and a fat lot of good either will be today against tanks and planes."

How true, how very true his prediction became. During the last war he again served, this time in the Home Guard, refusing a commission, choosing to remain a warrant officer serving his country in three wars spanning over forty years.

Father would get us back home before one o'clock and then we all sat down to Christmas dinner. There would be Grandmother and Grandfather, Mother and Father, Grandmother's elder brother and wife, Mother's two unmarried sisters and a cousin – eleven including Stewart and myself. Two tables would be placed end to end down the middle of the kitchen, covered with linen table cloths and laid with the best willow pattern china dinner service, the plates big enough to hold half a bucketful. The meat consisted of a brace of chicken and a large joint of sirloin; there was always a great variety of vegetables (Grandfather was a keen gardener); bread sauce, apple sauce, horse radish sauce and Yorkshire pudding completed the main course. Everything, with the exception of the beef, was home produced. Then followed Christmas pudding and mince pies, but somehow the mince pies never seemed to be touched.

After dinner the port came out for the adults and they settled down to an afternoon of blissful contentment. We tried out our new toys, had a nose round Grandfather's workshop, then a ride round the loose box on Grandmother's cob. (This was forbidden as her cob was always on the quick side, but on Christmas afternoon the chances of getting caught were very slim.) By late afternoon the grown-ups surfaced and as dusk appeared the lamps were lit: mantle-type lamps similar in design to the modern Tilley lanterns were placed on the kitchen table and in the front room; a lamp with a wick sat on a bracket in the hall. The cob was fed and bedded down, we had a cup of tea and a piece of Christmas cake and awaited the arrival of the rest of the family. Just after six Grandmother's young brother, his wife and unmarried son and daughter arrived. They lived at the other end of the village, where they milked a dairy herd and retailed the milk; they also ran the local mill. Then the quick clip-clop of Uncle Ern's cob could be heard coming down the road, steadying as he turned into the side entrance and came round to the back; like his mother he always drove a smart horse which not only pulled the trap but also carried him hunting once a week during most of the winter.

We would slip out the back door, picking up the hurricane lantern that had been lit in readiness; Uncle Ern would hand the reins to his wife, jump down and hold the cob while she descended, unbuckle the straps and take the horse into the stable, unharness him and tie him up in the spare stall where Grandfather had placed a feed of hay; then indoors we would go and join the rest of the party in the front room. This was another large room with blue flagstone floor covered with mats and rugs, an open wood fire burning in the hearth and the solitary lamp dimly illuminating the far corners. The large Christmas tree stood in one corner with a heap of parcels around its base – a present for everyone. The sideboard glinted with an array of glasses and bottles containing almost everything from whisky and port to elderflower and parsnip wine. Once everyone was settled with a drink we were allowed to light the two dozen or so candles on the tree. The lamp was turned down and, as the glasses were drained, the conversation began to flow. As befitted our age and the times, we were expected to be seen and not heard.

Farming topics dominated the conversation – what the hay had turned out like, how the cows were milking, what a grand bunch of heifers someone had – interspersed with local gossip and scandal. Mid-way through the evening the presents were given out by Grandmother, then at nine o'clock we went back into the kitchen for supper. There was ham at one end of the table and cold sirloin of beef at the other; three plates piled high with thick slices of bread cut from cottage loaves; and right in the middle of the table a truckle of Cheddar cheese with its bandage removed, the rind lightly scraped and rubbed over with a cloth, glowing yellow like a full moon in the lamplight. It would be one that either Aunt Edith had brought back from Wedmore or that her sister, Aunt Rose, had sent up from Dorset. It was not any old cheese, but one of the best from the previous season, having been made during the first ten days of June.

The ham and beef, helped down with a selection of home-made pickles and chutneys, soon disappeared, and then the company focused their attention on the cheese. I did not appreciate this ritual at the time but I suppose that around the table there would have been half a dozen of the best cheese makers in the area, perhaps in the county. Grandmother's elder brother would lead off with the question: "What is it going to cut like this round, then, Mary Ann?" Grandmother would get up from her place and from a pocket in her white starched pinafore produce a cheese sampler in its leather case. The sampler had a very thin blade about four inches long, half an inch broad at the handle and running down to a point. She slipped this into the top of the cheese and let it stay for a second or two while she felt the cheese with the ball of her thumb. The sample was removed, held under her nose and sniffed. She would then pronounce judgement, which could vary from "It's a tiny bit strong" to "Now this is something special." The truckle was cut and handed around with the port. There was always trifle and jelly to follow, which no one seemed to eat, with the exception of two small boys, who

31

were able to make pigs of themselves. At about half past ten the party broke up, for several of its members had to be up by five o'clock the next morning to do the milking. Farming never stops, not even for Christmas, and, as the hoofbeats of Uncle Ern's cob faded into the distance, another Christmas Day came to a close.

Very often, at this time of year, the corn ricks were threshed out. The threshing machine (which belonged to a contractor) was pulled and driven by a steam traction engine. It was quite a complicated piece of machinery. It removed the grain from the ears, then separated the grain from the straw and chaff and finally graded the corn into First, Second and Tailcorn. When threshing a good crop one could get an output of between fifteen and twenty four-bushel sacks per hour of oats (weighing one-and-a-half cwt), barley (two cwt) and wheat (two-and-a-quarter cwt). Two men came with the outfit: the driver, who was in charge and whose job it was to keep an even head of steam on the engine, see that the machine was threshing clean and keep all the bearings oiled; and his mate, who fed the corn into the drum and used to steer the engine when moving from farm to farm. These engines consumed over two hundred gallons of water a day and burned about six hundredweight of coal.

It took a further gang of six or eight to man the outfit: two men were required to pitch the sheaves from the rick onto the top of the thresher, another to cut the bonds, one more to sack the grain off, two making the straw and one raking chaff. (The boy always got this job.) Though not difficult, it was dirty work keeping the chaff clear from under the machine. You worked all day engulfed in a thick cloud of dust and by evening you were as black as the Ace of Spades. After a time I was promoted to bond cutter. The men on the corn rick pitched the sheaves onto the thresher with the butt ends outwards. I picked them up one at a time with my left hand and passed them on to the feeder who stood next to me, facing the open drum on the top of the machine. The string was cut with the knife held in the right hand and the feeder then shook the sheaf out into the drum. The sheaves had to be cut and passed quickly to the feeder so that he could keep a continuous flow of corn going through the machine. As long as this was done, the machine emitted a deep hum like a giant bumble bee. If a bond was cut too quickly and a sheaf dropped into the drum in one lump, the machine gave a great grunt which usually brought an enraged roar from the driver. Making a thresher grunt was an offence similar to driving over a sheaf of corn.

When threshing wheat from straw which was going to be used for thatching, instead of an elevator being fixed to the back of the machine to take the loose straw onto the rick, a trusser was used which tied the straw into large bundles with two strings. These bundles were known as "liners" and from them thatch was made. Just after a start had been made, Uncle Bert and the driver would go around to the back of the outfit where the threshed straw was pouring out and feel the ears. If any grain had been left in, they would shout to the feeder, and hold up an ear in one hand. This meant that the feeder had to slow down a bit. Then they came round to the front and examined the sample of grain as it ran down into the sacks. There were no moisture meters for testing the grain in those days, the yardstick being that if a man's hand and arm could be pushed into a sack of grain, it was dry enough to store in sacks. If not, it had to be shot out on the barn floor and kept turned for a week or two. It was a dirty job which no one liked very much but it was made bearable by a supply of free cider. The casual labourers who, among other jobs, followed the thresher from farm to farm, would refuse to work without their free cider.

Although most of the cows were dry and there were not many to milk, it was at this time of year that I enjoyed milking most. How pleasant it was to go into a snug, warm shed at six o'clock on a cold, wet December morning to find the cows bedded up knee deep with clean straw and chewing away at sweet-scented hay. You fetched your bucket and stool and sat down under the first cow, pressing your head into her warm flank; the milk frothed into the bucket. You listened to the rain on the roof and thought of the wonderful cooked breakfast you would be getting in about an hour's time. School was still a fortnight away and life seemed very good.

By the Easter holiday the pattern had changed again. All the cows had calved down and were in full milk. They were still housed and being fed hay and, now that they were freshly calved, quite a lot of linseed and cotton cake. This used to come in large slabs, which were put through a cake cracker to break them down into small pieces. About the middle of April, when the grass had grown sufficiently, the cows were turned out. This pleased everyone for now, instead of having to feed, water and clean them out all the time, they did it for themselves. Also, the milk yield would increase by anything up to twenty-five per cent. There was, and still is, nothing like April grass for producing milk and producing it cheaply. The cows were as pleased as the farm staff that they were being turned out; for some four months they had been housed and fed a rather monotonous diet of hay, cake and water. Now they were free again, with the sun shining on their backs and fresh, young grass underfoot. For the first few days of this new freedom, their walk back to the fields after milking had lost its old, slow, gentle amble; it now had a sense of urgency about it. As soon as they reached the field, their heads went down and they began grazing straight away. When they had eaten until they could eat no more, they lay down under the trees in a state of utter contentment, chewing the cud with half-closed eyes – oblivious to anything going on around them.

It was against this family and village background that my brother and I were brought up. In 1936, he was apprenticed to a building firm in Bath and in the spring of 1939 I left school and went to live with my Uncle and Aunt in Dorset. It was in September of that year that a former Austrian Corporal heaved a spanner in the works and this tranquil, self-contained village way of life received a shock from which it never recovered. Overnight many of the young men disappeared into the Army and Navy reserve, Yeomanry and Territorials. Shortly afterwards, the village opened its arms to mothers and children evacuated from London. Within a few months several of the big houses in the village were commandeered by the Army and the troops moved in. Villagers watched the vapour trails in the sky as part of the Battle of Britain was fought over their heads. They listened to the drone of enemy bombers overhead in the night and saw the glow in the sky as Bath and Bristol burned. With the help of Land Army girls they set about their war effort of producing food, and in spite of shortages of equipment, feedstuffs and labour, they did just that.

After nearly six long years the war came to an end. The evacuees and troops departed, the land girls disappeared and the young men came home. But, like some of her sons, pre-war village life never did return.

Pre-War Farming

FARMING in the thirties was conducted at a more leisurely pace than it is today, although much more physical manual work was involved. The pace was determined by the motive power (which was still being provided by the horse) and the amount of labour then employed in the industry. The demise of the heavy horse and the subsequent drastic reduction in the labour force have accounted for most of the dramatic changes that have taken place in farming during my lifetime.

Without a doubt the tractor has revolutionised the industry more than any other single thing. Until the last war there were relatively few tractors in use on the smaller farms of Dorset and Somerset, and these tractors bore little resemblance to their modern counterparts, being basically an engine, transmission and four wheels. They had no hydraulics, lights, self-starters or cabs and in many cases were mounted on steel wheels. The older generation of farmers and farmworkers, especially the carters, regarded them with scorn and mistrust and were very quick to point out their failings. But forgetting their advantages, I remember my Uncle's warning when he took delivery of his first tractor. As a young lad I was highly delighted, thinking that now I should be able to ride all day instead of walking behind horses, but the old boy was far from convinced that he had made a good investment and I was told rather forcibly to remember: "Every time you starts that damn thing you be costing I money." The fact that the horse had to be fed did not come into his reckoning; they ate what the farm produced, whereas the petrol and TVO had to be bought. Every time he had to write a cheque for it he used to complain.

Many of the workers were of the same mind, if for a different reason. Our old rick maker summed it up one evening after a hard day ricking hay that had been swept in by a tractor sweep: "The trouble with this yer box of tricks is it don't get tired. Horses be like men; they slows up as the day goes on – this damn thing don't." The innovation of the tractor was one of the first steps that led the industry to being much less self-supporting. Mechanisation also led to a huge reduction in the amount of labour directly employed within farming and an increase in that engaged in the industries that serviced agriculture. When the power units were horses, and before that oxen, the industry had bred all its own power units and replacements – farmers either breeding their own colts or buying them as broken or unbroken horses from other farmers. Besides supplying horses for agriculture there had been, and still was right up to the war, a thriving trade in selling heavy horses for town work. For many farmers it was part of the farm income; they broke in several colts a year, worked them for two or three years on the farm and then sold them on for town work at about double what they had cost as unbroken colts. The only expense they would have incurred would have been the blacksmith's bill for shoeing and their keep, whilst all the time they would have been supplying the power for the farm. You cannot buy a tractor, work it for two years and then sell it for double what it cost!

A horse working on the land would wear out about four sets of shoes a year, a lot more if it was employed on road work. The general pattern was to start with a new set of shoes which were removed after about six weeks when the hoof would have grown somewhat. The hoof was trimmed back and the shoes replaced. After about another six weeks they would be worn out and replaced with a new set. Shoeing colts for the first time could, on occasions, be a hazardous occupation. When an animal weighing three parts of a ton started to fling its legs about, something had to give. Most colts had their feet trimmed a time or two before being shod, which was done just after they had started to be broken in. After working them for several hours until they were tired they were taken to the blacksmith's shop. They generally stood, reasonably quietly, while their hooves were being trimmed and shaped to take the shoe but they sometimes played up a bit when the hot shoe was fitted and the smoke rose in clouds. The fun generally began, however, when the smith started to nail the shoe in place, using seven nails per shoe – three on one side, four on the other. As soon as he had managed to get four nails (two each side) into the first shoe he would drop the foot and everyone would partake of the cider that had been brought down to celebrate the occasion.

As a young man I drove horses with most of the farm implements and enjoyed doing so, but there has been a lot of sentimental twaddle written about working horses. It is one thing to play about with an odd horse or two and quite another to drive a team regularly. Our horses used to be stabled from early October until May and a carter's day went something like this: up in the stable at about half past five in the morning, give the horses a feed of chaff and corn which had been prepared the previous afternoon, clean out the stable (putting all the unused bedding under the manger), brush the horses over, then give them a drink and a second feed before having your own breakfast, harness up and be out of the stable ready to start work at seven o'clock. You then went to where you were working, shut into whichever implement you were using and worked until ten o'clock, when you stopped, put the nose bags on and had your own lunch. At half past ten you were off again and continued until two o'clock, when you shut out and went back to the stable. On arriving, you unharnessed the horses, fed them again and then went in for a late dinner. After dinner you cut the chaff for the next day, groomed your horses, bedded them down, gave them another feed and went home to tea at about five o'clock. At eight o'clock you had a last look round, racked up with hay and that was that. How many young men today would stick that week in, week out? In those days you had to, not because you particularly wanted to, but there was no other option.

The actual feeding of the work horses was fairly straightforward: oat straw cut into chaff and mixed with oats was the basic feed, with a feed of good hay in the racks last thing at night. During the winter and spring they were given either two or three whole mangolds in the manger, or these were pulped and mixed into their chaff and corn. The oat ration used to vary from farm to farm, but was generally between a sack and a sack and a half per week for three horses, plus any more that you could wangle. In those days quite a lot of linseed cake used to be fed to cattle and sheep and came in sheets three feet long, a foot wide and about one-and-a-half inches thick. These sheets were broken into small pieces by putting them through a cake cracker which consisted of a pair of spiked rollers that rotated into each sheet, breaking it into pieces from about the size of a walnut to that of a hazelnut, according to how close the rollers were set. Under the rollers, where the broken cake came out, there was a perforated grid down which the cake slid to be bagged up, separating the dust from the knobs of cake. This dust was much prized by the carters who would bag it up and add a handful or two to a horse's feed – and if the opportunity presented itself they would pinch some of the cake as well. It was wonderful stuff to make a horse's coat shine.

The carters took great pride, not only in the standard of work they did, but also in the condition and appearance of their horses. To this end, they would scrounge any extra feed they could get their hands on. Bill Hutchings, Uncle Bert's head carter, used to tell the story that at one farm where he worked the granary was situated above the cart shed. He drilled a hole in the granary floor under a hutch full of oats; the hole was just big enough to take a bottle cork. When racking up at night, he used to get into a wagon which was under the cork, remove the cork, fill a bucket with oats and replace the cork. This went on all one winter until he was found out, when, according to him, there was hell to pay.

Most of the older carters had their own harness trimmings: breast straps, bells, loin straps, leading reins and very often brass harness. When going to town to deliver corn to the railway station, or to fetch coal or feedstuff, they would always dress up the horses – manes braided, tails done up, the harness and brasses cleaned – the horses shining and covered with hammer marks, which are the shiny spots on a horse's ribs, loin and flanks when it is in first class condition.

On many farms the chaff cutter, cake cracker, mangold pulper and in some cases the elevator were driven not by a stationary petrol engine, but by a horse gear. This consisted of a metal frame, on which a cast iron crown wheel some three feet in diameter was mounted with the cogs downwards. Across the top of the crown wheel a four-inch square pole about ten feet long was bolted. This had a bodkin attached to the end, into which the horse's traces were hooked. A thin metal rod from the centre of the crown wheel was clipped onto the horse's bit and, as the horse walked forward, this rod kept it moving round and round in a circle, pulling the pole behind it, thus rotating the crown wheel which in turn drove a small pinion. A long shaft running along the ground was fixed to the pinion at one end and by means of a coupling to the barn machinery at the other. As the horse walked round on the end of the pole the crown wheel went round at the same speed but, because it was geared up, drove the pinion much faster, which in turn drove the shaft and then the machinery. At hay making or harvest the shaft was coupled to the drive of the elevator. As schoolboys we sometimes got the job of keeping the horse going round and round. Very often a horse new to the gear would repeatedly stop when coming up to the shaft that ran along the ground, so the easiest way to keep them going was to ride them round. The great drawback with this was that the horse was generally sweaty and you soon got a wet seat and a sore bottom.

Up to the mid-1950s many farms kept one or two horses to do light haulage jobs, especially for feeding cattle and sheep in the winter, but as these horses became old they were not replaced and the tractor took over completely. By this time many of the older petrol TVO tractors had been superseded by diesel models with self-starters which could be stopped and started at will, making them much more suitable for jobbing.

From that time onwards they seemed to develop into a farm taxi as well as a power unit. With the old iron-wheeled TVO tractors, you went out, say, ploughing, carried your lunch and dinner and ploughed all day. In the evening you sheeted up the tractor, then came back the next day and continued ploughing. TVO and petrol would be brought up with a horse and cart and you kept going, perhaps not taking the tractor home for a fortnight. Nowadays farmworkers go home to breakfast, dinner and tea and many of the dairymen use a tractor to fetch the cows.

A further reduction in farming self-sufficiency has been due to the universal use of flails for hedge cutting – a task that the tractor has revolutionised – coupled with the great number of hedges that have been pulled out to make bigger fields so the large, modern tractors can operate economically.

Apart from a few roadside hedges, which were trimmed by hand, most hedges used to be allowed to grow for from five to ten years and they would then be "made or laid". In West Dorset most of the hedges were what was known as "double": they were, in fact, two hedges on the top of a bank, and were some four feet high and upwards of six feet wide.

The first job when making the hedge was to trim out all the brambles, then dig up the bank. Generally, a ditch two spits wide and one deep was taken out and the earth put on top of the bank. Then the hedge was laid down. To do this, the sticks were cut nearly through, right down at their base, then pulled over so that they lay down flat on the newly dug bank. They were split down from where they were cut, leaving them connected to their stumps by a tongue of wood, through which the sap was able to flow, thereby keeping the stick alive. This was known as "plushing" and the sticks so laid were referred to as "plushers". These plushers were pinned down, the ditch shovelled out and the earth put in the middle of the hedge behind the plushers. With the double hedges, this procedure was carried out on both sides. The hedges consisted of a variety of woods, hazel being predominant, with some maple, hawthorn, blackthorn and ash stools or mocks. When laid, the hedge would be stock proof and, with its high bank, would form a windbreak for cattle that were being out-wintered. The hazel, maple and thorn would be some ten feet long when laid and the ash up to twenty feet.

Hedge laying took place in the winter and early spring when the leaves were off the wood and before the sap started to rise. Most of the laying was done by piece work. The rate just before the war was six to eight shillings a chain to lay and dig one side; eight to ten shillings if both sides were dug; faggots and pea sticks were paid for at two old pence a bundle.

There were several important by-products from this hedge laying. The long, straight hazel rods were cut out for spar gads. From these, thatching spars were made to fix the thatch firmly on the hay ricks, corn ricks and thatched buildings and houses. These gads were about five to six feet long and one-and-a-half to two inches in diameter. They were split down into halves and then into quarters, each end was sharpened to a point and they were twisted in the middle to form what looked like a giant wooden staple. Making the spars was quite a skilled job, which was generally carried out during the winter by the thatchers. They used to sit on an old chair or stool, lay the gad across their knees and, starting at the top, split the gad with a very small hook which was twisted first upwards and then downwards to keep the split running down the centre of the gad. Using the same technique, they split the halves into quarters and, with three flicks of the wrist, they were sharpened. They would keep at it until the middle of the afternoon and then proceed to twist them up, sticking them into a bundle of thatch as they did so. The spars were tied into bundles of fifty, two of which would be jammed point to point to make one hundred. On a good day, a spar maker with straight gads could make one thousand.

The smaller hazel rods were tied in bundles and used as pea and bean sticks. The brushwood from the hazel, ash and other wood (with the exception of thorn and brambles) was tied into faggots. These were large bundles of wood about four feet long and tied in the middle with a hazel bond. The bigger wood, or leg wood, was used as firewood and supplied virtually all the fuel for the farm kitchen. The long, straight ash poles were frequently used for fencing rails and posts. The faggots were often used as the staddle, or foundation, for hay and corn ricks, which kept the bottom of the rick above ground level, thus avoiding damage to the base from damp. After they had served this purpose, they were used as firewood.

Most farmhouses at that time had a large fire in the hearth and many still had bread ovens. Agas and Rayburns, like tractors, had not yet become common. Those old, open fires burnt only wood (and quite a lot of it), with many remaining permanently alight. The wood was placed on a pair of fire dogs which were about two feet apart and kept the fire a couple of inches above the hearth. A large log was always placed at the back and the smaller wood in front of it. These big logs were known as "back sticks" and a good one would last a couple of days. Most of the wood was not cut up into short lengths but left in four-feet long pieces. When they burnt through in the centre, the ends would be thrown into the middle to finish burning. Hanging down over the fire would be a couple of chains with hooks on the end, from which a kettle or cast iron crock pot could be hung. You would come down early in the morning, rake the ashes over, then put on half a dry faggot, which had been brought in the night before and stood beside the fireplace in readiness. A few puffs with the bellows and within minutes you had a roaring fire which engulfed the kettle in flames and brought it to the boil for your early cup of tea – not as easy or as clean as the electric kettle, but almost as fast.

One of our neighbours, who had an open fire and a bread oven, used to buy coal only for threshing. His sister baked her own bread, always on Fridays, and it was as fresh the following Thursday as any day-old bread is today. I used to give them a hand with the hay making and harvest on occasions. The dinner was always cooked in the iron crock pot; the potatoes, peas, beans or carrots were put into nets and cooked all together. There was very often a boiled pudding as well. On Fridays we always had a miniature cottage loaf for tea. While still hot from the oven, the top was broken off and a walnut-sized knob of butter was put on, which melted into the warm bread. This was followed by a large slice of apple cake with raisins – food fit for a king!

The tractor has undoubtedly taken the hard work out of manure carting and spreading. Before hydraulics became standard equipment on tractors, manure handling was a very labour-intensive operation. In the days of the horse it was hauled in two-wheeled carts called putts, which could be tipped up. The putts were loaded by hand using four-tine dung forks, then pulled up to where the manure was to be spread and put out in heaps, six yards apart, in lines right across the field. The lines were also spaced at six-yard intervals. To unload, the tailboard was first removed and then the load tipped up a little way. You had to be careful, for if tipped too high the whole load slipped out in one great heap. Using a dung crook (a four-tine pick with tines turned down at right angles to the stem), enough manure for a heap was pulled out. Six yards further on, the process was repeated and so on until the putt was empty. On pasture, there were seven heaps to the load, but when manuring arable land for root crops, there were only four – almost twice as thick on arable as on pasture. After being heaped out, the manure had to be broken into small pieces with a dung fork and spread out evenly. Nowadays, with a fore-end loader and manure spreaders, things are very different: the manure is loaded into the spreader in a few minutes and spread just as quickly, with all the work being done from the tractor seat.

By and large there were few farm tasks for which I preferred horses to tractors, but the one that stands out a mile is ploughing. There is no occupation so satisfying as ploughing behind a good pair of horses – one horse walking the furrow, the other on the unploughed land – accompanied by the clink of trace chains, the creak of bodkins and way bar as they take the strain and the occasional grate as the shear or coulter scrapes along the odd stone or flint. The shear and coulter cut a furrow ten inches wide and five inches deep. As the skim coulter slides off a ribbon of soil on the near side of the furrow, the soil rises on the breast, gradually turning on its edge as it follows the turn-furrow back, until it is finally pressed over and almost inverted, with not a blade of grass or stubble showing. A plough, when set properly, would stay in its work without the handles being held. I can still see Bill Hutchings on the plough: with the reins hung on the handles, he would start off up the field, let go the handles, get out his pipe, fill it from his pouch, light up and when it was going to his satisfaction, take hold of the handles in time to turn the outfit at the top of the field. He would plough all day and rarely ever touch a rein, his team turning to the left or right in response to his "Come here" or "Hook off".

Hay making, especially on dairy farms, was a much more important operation then. There was virtually no silage made at that time, so hay was the main winter feedstuff for cattle. The conventional grass cutters were pulled by two horses working side by side on a pole, which cut a swathe four feet six inches wide. The actual cutting was done by a reciprocating knife running inside the cutter bar. These knives had to be sharpened repeatedly with a file and you could always tell when the knives were blunt, because the horses had to pull much harder. There were also single-horse mowers which cut three feet six inches wide. These were generally used by a few small farmers and were very hard work for one horse, hence they were known as "horse killers". A single-horse machine which cut the regulation four feet six was brought out in the thirties but the knife was driven by an air-cooled engine. They were reasonably successful but, because of the extra weight of the engine, they were still hard work for a single horse. During the war, many of the horse machines were converted to be drawn by tractor, then tractor trailer machines came in, followed by hydraulic lift, power-driven knife bars. These have, in turn, been superseded by large drum mowers which cut up to twelve feet wide.

After cutting, the practice was to leave the hay in swathe for several days until it had dried half way through. This differs greatly from the modern practice where hay is beaten with power-operated turners within hours of cutting, in an effort to get it fit to bale in a shorter time. This is achieved, without a doubt, but at the loss of much of the leaf which is the best part of the hay. The half-dry swathes used to be turned over by swathe turners pulled by a single horse, turning two swathes at once, but instead of kicking and flinging the hay all over the place like the modern turners they gently rolled it over like a great long ribbon. If the weather was good the hay was very often turned only once and then made into rows with a side rake. This machine, like the swathe turner, was pulled by one horse. It went up the field, rolling two swathes into one, then back down putting two more into the first two, making new rows of four swathes, ready for sweeping or loading into wagons.

There were two types of horse-drawn hay sweeps. The smaller type, pulled by a single horse, had short teeth which were bolted onto a beam with a pair of handles in the centre and a long chain trace on each end attached to the horse's harness. The horse walked alongside the row of hay, pulling the sweep behind and you lifted the handles so that the teeth ran under the hay and picked it up. When the sweep was full, it was driven to the elevator, stopped and the sweep pulled back a foot or two. The handles were pushed up until the sweep was balanced on top of the teeth. The horse moved forward, rolling the sweep right over the top of the load. When sweeping, care had to be taken not to hold the handles too high or the teeth would stick in the ground and either break off a tooth or tip the sweep over. The much larger, two-horse sweeps had teeth some ten feet long. They had wheels fixed to the end of the beam to keep the teeth at the correct angle to the ground and a seat for the driver. The horses were harnessed, one each side, on a pole. To empty the sweep the horses had to walk backwards and push the sweep out from under its load. Tractor sweeps were almost the same, but the sweep was attached to the tractor front axle and there were no wheels or seat.

The rick gang for sweeping consisted of five men: two pitching the hay into the elevator and three on the rick. The rick maker worked round and round the outside of the rick, with a second man fitting in behind him and the third passing the hay to them from where the elevator dropped it in the middle of the rick. One of the disadvantages of sweeping was that the hay had to be ricked in the field where it had grown. This was all right if it could be fed right there to out-wintered stock, but as much of the hay was fed indoors to housed cattle that meant hauling it back to the building in the winter. Quite a lot of hay was hauled back to the farm building in wagons, therefore, and ricks were put up in the rick yard, situated alongside the cowsheds, from where it could be cut out and carried straight in to the cows.

Some farms had hay loaders which, when pulled behind the wagons, picked up the hay and pushed it up and over the back of the wagon. It was hard work loading behind one of these, with one man pushing the hay forward and a second making the load, and very difficult to work while maintaining your balance on a wagon which swayed and pitched as the load got bigger. The wagon had wooden wheels with iron tyres and no springs, so you felt every bump in the ground. A lot of hay was pitched by hand. The wagons would go between two rows with a pitcher on either side and the horse would move up every time a pitcher drew level with its head. A shout to the loader always preceded the command to the horse. To move without the time honoured shout of "Hold fast" was considered a cardinal sin. The outfit then moved up some ten or a dozen yards, stopping and waiting for the pitchers to work up level again. Leading the horse was always a job much sought after by schoolboys. Pitching was slower than the hay loader, but much more civilised, especially for the loader.

There was very little wastage in those days. After the crop was gathered the field would be horse raked, the rakings picked up and the lines raked clean. The ricks were raked down and then tucked or pulled, which entailed pulling all the loose hay from the sides and ends of the ricks; this stopped the weather spoiling the outside. They were then thatched with long, straight wheat straw, firmly pegged down with spars and, on their foundation of faggots, they were impervious to rain, wind or snow.

The corn harvest was even more different in those days. Combines were unheard of and all the corn was cut, ricked and threshed. Cutting with a binder was one of the hardest tasks the horses had to do. Three horses worked a six-foot binder which cut, tied and dropped the sheaves in order by rows. The machine was land-driven from the main centre wheel and by means of sprocket and chain the knife, fans, bed canvas, elevator canvas, packer, knatter and trip were propelled to turn all this machinery. Pulling the machine was hard work, which accounts for the fact that binders were quickly adapted to be drawn by tractor power.

Up until the beginning of the Second World War, nearly all the cornfields were mown around the edges by scythe before the binder was allowed in. If this was not done, the binder had to be driven, first time round, through the standing corn, trampling out quite a lot of the grain. Until the war made labour scarce, it was considered poor farming practice not to open by hand. Frank Parker, who worked for Uncle Bert, could mow around a corn field at almost walking pace, leaving the severed stalks of grain lying perfectly straight, so they could be gathered up and tied neatly with little trouble. You picked them up until there were enough for a sheaf, then banged the butt end on the ground to level the end of the sheaf. Five or six stalks were pulled out by the ears, passed around the middle, pulled tight and then, holding the ears in the left hand, the bottom end of the stalks was passed right around the ears and the end tucked under the bond to form a strong binding for the sheaf.

Old Frank had been a mower in his youth when a lot of the grass, and particularly barley, had been cut by scythe. He could balance his scythe on two fingers of each hand, then swing it, seemingly without effort, through corn or grass and mow a swathe of seven feet. He told me once that the best mower he ever worked with he left behind before dinner. I assumed that he meant he was the better man. "No, no," he replied. "He were better at it than I but he couldn't whet." Every now and then Frank would stop, stand his scythe on the end of its handle and, taking his whetstone from its holder at the back of his belt, he would sharpen up. Holding the scythe blade with his left hand and taking the whetstone in his right, he would draw the stone down alternate sides of the blade, making it ring with every stroke. A dozen such strokes and it could cut like a razor.

As soon as the corn was cut the sheaves were stood in stooks of eight or ten sheaves and left to dry out. Sometimes, especially with under-sown barley, the grass and clover would be nearly as high as the corn. When this happened, it would be run through the binder loose and not tied into sheaves, but turned by hand and hauled loose. In a wet spell, when the sheaves had become soaked repeatedly, the strings were cut to facilitate drying and again the crop was carted loose; but loose corn was always more difficult and expensive to handle. Harvesting with this system was extremely labour-intensive and much more at the mercy of the weather, because most corn was left in stook for five or six days and oats for up to a fortnight.

The oats were cut when the straw was still green and allowed to ripen in stooks, which increased the feeding value of the straw. Straw was a very valuable by-product and played an important part in a mixed farm economy. The long, straight wheat straw was used for thatching, not only for the hay and corn ricks, but for cottages and farm buildings as well. The best oat and barley straw was used for feeding and vast quantities of all three were utilised for bedding down the horses, cattle, pigs and, at lambing time, the sheep. Virtually none was burned. Besides all the work the actual harvesting entailed – cutting, stitching, hauling, ricking and thatching – there was still the dirty, dusty threshing to be done during the winter and those great four-bushel sacks to be loaded and unloaded. After a couple of hours at the end of the day spent carrying them up the granary steps you were ready for tea and bed.

The combine may have taken the picture-book romance out of the harvest but it has also removed a lot of hard, back-breaking and dusty work – and a lot of the uncertainty. Once the corn has been cut and the grain is in the tank, it is safe from the elements, instead of having to stand in the field at the mercy of the weather before it is fit to haul.

Forty cows were considered to be a large dairy, many consisting of just a dozen or twenty. The predominant breed was Dairy Shorthorns and milking was done by hand, which meant a milker for every dozen or so cows. In addition to the winter feed of hay, concentrates were given – some in the form of compounds – but a lot of linseed and cotton cake was still being used. Many of the dry cows and young stock were out-wintered, with only the milking cows being housed. Most farms kept a bull. Artificial insemination, or "the bull in the bowler hat", was unheard of. My Uncle always insisted that a stout stick be carried if a bull, no matter how quiet, was running with the cows. He maintained that it was always the quiet bulls that did the damage as you were always on your guard for the bad-tempered ones. The quiet bulls were taken for granted and familiarity bred contempt. One must remember that in those days no cattle were dehorned; the only ones without horns were the natural polls, Aberdeen Angus and Red Polls, mostly.

In this part of the country quite a large number of farmers still made cheese, right up to the start of the last war, when the shortage of labour and the demand for milk for liquid consumption virtually put an end to the industry. Today there are still what is known as farmhouse cheese makers, but these are more like factory enterprises, processing several thousand gallons of milk daily compared to less than a hundred then.

Before the advent of the Milk Marketing Board in the

mid-thirties, farmers used to negotiate their own contract annually with a dairy, some of the milk going for manufacture but a large part for liquid consumption. Much of the milk, contained in churns, was collected from the farms by lorry and railed to London from Frome and Westbury. I can remember when the old, tapered-sided seventeen-gallon churns were in use. These were superseded by twelve-gallon churns, still tapered; and then by the straight-sided ten galloners, which were used until bulk tanker collection took over. The old seventeen galloners used to weight nearly two hundredweight when full. In the late thirties, Express Dairy built a new depot at Frome station, from where the milk was transported to London in rail tankers. That was, I suppose, the beginning of the end of the milk churn.

Dairy farming at that time was about the only branch of agriculture that was at all profitable. There was a considerable swing to this type of farming and quite a lot of arable land was sown down. As piped water became more readily available, it enabled more of this former arable land to be used for dairying. There was also a change from the predominant spring calving herds for cheese making, to more autumn calving to supply the liquid demand, which was constant all year round.

One of Mother's uncles, who farmed a couple of miles from our home, changed his farming policy in this way. Uncle John Hill was a remarkable man in many ways. When he got married in the late 1880s he took on the Rising Sun public house, with about twenty acres of land on the Mendips, where he used to keep six cows. Aunt Liza looked after the pub by day and milked the cows. The milk was sent down to Croscombe, where her mother farmed, to be made into cheese. During the day, Uncle John used to haul coal from the pits at Radstock to Wells on a tonnage basis; he once told me that he made quite a lot of money doing this. The standard outfit consisted of a road wagon and a pair of horses, but Uncle always drove three horses with a colt in the middle and an extra ton of coal up. Besides the extra coal he carried, he used to have a couple of broken horses to sell each year. He always said that it was while doing this that he learned two lessons regarding livestock, which influenced his entire life – to buy the best and to feed it well. By the end of the First World War he was a tenant farmer with some two hundred acres on the Mendips, milking two dairies, the output of which was made into cheese.

In the early 1920s Uncle John bought a farm on the Somerset/Wiltshire borders – some twenty miles away. The day they moved they milked the cows on the Mendips in the morning, then walked them up and milked them in their new home in the evening. He continued making cheese until 1927 and then began selling milk to London on a maximum/minimum contract. He would put the milk on the train every evening at Westbury station – a drive of a couple of miles with the cob and a milk float – not much of a job on a pouring wet winter evening, with only candle lanterns on the float. Although he changed his way of selling milk and moved from summer production to a regular, consistent output throughout the year, there were many things he never changed. He always had at least one horse over and above what the farm could justify. If a neighbour was looking for a good horse Uncle John always had one for sale and promptly put a colt in its place.

The local horse dealer cottoned on to Uncle John's weakness for a good colt: whenever he had an outstanding one, it was put in a field in front of his house, alongside the road, where the old boy would be sure to see it on his way to market on Wednesdays. Aunt Liza lost count of the times he returned from market with a colt tied onto the back of the gig. Another practice he never changed was the number of calves reared for replacement, always keeping every heifer calf born. This meant that he had more heifers than he required coming into the dairy each year. He used to sell a dozen or fifteen freshly calved young cows annually, generally third calvers. Over the years, he built up a great reputation as a vendor of genuine young cows, for he was an extremely good feeder and his cattle used to be in really first class condition. They were generally purchased by one or other of the local producer-retailers, many of whom bought in the best young cows they could find, first because they gave more milk than a heifer and second (because the milk was sold retail at a much higher price), they could afford to pay more.

Once, when I was staying with Uncle John whilst on half-term holiday, he took me to Frome market and that particular day he had a grand third-calf, strawberry roan cow for sale. The previous Friday she had produced a heifer calf. Because Uncle John always retained the heifers, she went to market without her calf, which had been taken away from her the previous afternoon. It was general practice, however, to sell freshly calved heifers or cows with their calves at foot. This allowed the buyer to see that the cow had had a full-term calf and, by the size of the calf, how long ago she had calved.

At about four o'clock, this cow was stripped right out. She was not milked that morning and at about nine o'clock a lorry arrived, she was loaded up, a truss of straw and a bundle of hay going with her. We set off for market shortly after, with the cob in the gig. Uncle John drove straight to the market, where we found the cow tied up with the others that were for sale, bedded up and eating hay. The night before her tail and udder had been clipped, and that morning a market porter had washed her down. She looked a picture. During the next couple of hours, several potential buyers came to look her over, feeling the skin over her ribs to see if it was nice and slack (a tight skin was said to denote an unsound beast). Then they would try her udder, squeezing a squirt out of each teat in turn; this was in the days of hand milking and no one wanted a cow that was hard to milk. They would then feel around the udder to make sure that all her quarters were even. Questions were asked about her age, if she was quiet and where her calf was. Uncle John answered all their questions and always finished with the same remark: "I warrant her right and straight in every way."

Several heifers and calves were sold first and then into the ring she came. Uncle John walked in with her and stood up beside the auctioneer, Charlie Cooper, who gave out the particulars. "Now gentlemen; this is the one you have been waiting for. We don't see John Hill too often, but when we do, he always brings a cracker. Today is no exception: a grand, young cow, right in her prime, warranted everything right; and she calved last Friday. Start me at thirty guineas." Someone started her at twenty-five and up the bidding went to thirty, where it hung for a moment. Charlie Cooper proceeded to extol her virtues: "Look at the colour, gentlemen, and what a bag!" Uncle John walked over and, bending down, proceeded to milk a few squirts from all four teats. "There you are; quiet as a baby and easy as a glove," continued the auctioneer. Off went the bidding again and at thirty-three-and-a-half guineas the hammer came down.

As he left the ring, John Hill lifted his hat to the auctioneer and said: "Thank you, Mr Cooper; thank you, gentlemen." It was something that impressed me at the time and I have copied it all my life. Even to this day, as I thank the auctioneer and the company on leaving the ring, my memory flashes back to Uncle John Hill and that day at Frome market, some fifty odd years ago.

In many ways, Uncle John was ahead of his time. Quite a few of the things he did, which were unusual at the time, have become accepted practice today. He was a much heavier feeder of concentrates than most farmers of his day and always fed cake to the in-calf heifers and dry cows that were springing to calf – a practice that is taken for granted now – but at that time very few people indulged in it. In fact, the opposite was the case and most dry cows were fed only straw and second class hay right up to the time they calved. For many years, he used only roan Dairy Shorthorn bulls, which were sent down from Cumberland. He was never over-stocked and always had at least a couple of ricks of good hay left over at the end of the winter. One could say that he specialised. The whole farm was down to grass and the entire enterprise geared to producing milk and rearing dairy replacements. The only cattle he ever bought was the occasional bull. He rarely had a horse on the farm over six years old, so all his livestock was either earning or growing into money.

To many people, rabbits conjure up an image of cuddly, furry creatures, but before myxomatosis virtually destroyed them they were, in this part of the country, a very destructive pest. It was a difficult job to assess fully the damage they did to pastures that were being grazed, but on the arable fields and those laid up for hay, the destruction was there for all to see. They used to nibble their way into a crop (especially corn) and eat a wide swathe all around a field – and they bred very rapidly. A doe would have several litters of young each year, a number of which would, in turn, breed that same year. Because of the rate at which they multiplied, it was essential – in the interests of good farming – that their numbers were kept under control. Besides having to keep rabbits under control from a farming standpoint, I used to have a vested interest, when a young man, in catching them. They represented a considerable part of my income, for I was permitted to keep, for pocket money, the earnings from any rabbits I caught on the farm. After a while I became quite adept at the job!

From September to March, Sundays were generally spent ferreting. We used to work like mad on Sunday mornings to get all our jobs finished before breakfast and just after nine o'clock, loaded up with ferret boxes, nets, a spade and a gun apiece, we would set off. Most of the burrows were in the hedge banks and two people were needed, one each side of the bank. The actual burrow varied from half a dozen holes to over fifty. After quietly placing a net over every hole and two or three in the middle of the hedge, the ferret was put in and we stood back a few yards and waited. Suddenly, there would be a thump, thump as a rabbit kicked out with its back feet on being disturbed by the ferret; within a second or two it generally bolted out of the burrow at top speed, only to become enmeshed in one of the nets. He would be grabbed and, with a quick blow with the side of the hand, his neck was dislocated, killing him instantly. Then the net was reset and we waited for the ferret to bolt another one out. Occasionally a rabbit escaped from a hole that had been missed when netting or he got around the side of the net and raced off across the field. Up came the gun and – with a bit of luck – he would be rolled over first shot. If you pulled twice and missed, that was sixpence for the cartridges down the drain and two bob for the rabbit gone west. The loss of half a crown was a serious business. Every now and then a rabbit refused to bolt and would get up in an end hole with the ferret behind it. When this happened, it had to be dug out. A second ferret, wearing a collar with a line attached, was sent in to locate its mate; then you dug along following the line until the rabbit could be reached and pulled out.

This sounds quite a bloodthirsty business; but ferreting

was one of the most humane ways of keeping the rabbit population down. We used to enjoy ourselves, as well as providing ourselves with pocket money. I used to reckon to finance my courting out of the rabbit money! On a good Sunday, we would catch up to thirty and get back to dinner by two o'clock, after which there was the feeding up and the afternoon milking to be done.

Long netting was another method we used. The nets were either fifty or one hundred yards long and three feet high, with two cords, one threaded in the mesh along the bottom and one along the top of the net. They were held up by pointed hazel sticks, two feet long and as big around as a person's little finger, spaced every five or six yards. To run the net out you pegged down the end, then paced it out inserting the hazel sticks a few inches into the ground as you went, pulling the top cord tight and fixing it with a half-hitch to the top of the stick. When all the net was out and fixed on the sticks, the end was pegged down. It took quite a lot of practice to be able to accomplish this quietly and at speed in the dark, for long netting always took place at night, when you could not be seen by the rabbits. (By this time they would have left their burrows and be well out in the field.) The net was run out between the burrows and the feeding rabbits and once erected in place, you got round in front and drove them back towards their burrows – and into the net they went. A dark, windy night was vital for success, running the net downwind of the quarry, so that they heard no sound. On a good, rough night it was possible to run out the net two or three times in different places, the catch varying from the odd one or two to over twenty each time. It was quite common to catch between forty and fifty rabbits in an evening.

So much has been written about the good old days before the war, but I often wonder how good they really were for many farmworkers and their families. Those employed in agriculture today are considered to be towards the bottom of the pay scale, yet we have a standard of living that could never have been imagined before the war. Wages for day men in the early 1930s were about thirty-two shillings for fifty hours, but the stockmen were paid another three or four shillings for longer hours, including Sundays.

Many of the married men had a free cottage with the job or paid a small rent of a shilling or two. The majority of these cottages had none of the facilities which we take for granted today. Many were two up and two down with a lean-to back house, containing the copper. The downstairs rooms had flagstone floors with a cast iron, black-leaded kitchen stove as the only means of cooking. There was no electricity, gas or piped water, a well or outside pump being shared by several families. The toilets were at the bottom of the garden and contained either a bucket or vault which had to be emptied periodically. Bathrooms or hot water systems were unheard of – the copper in the back house was used to heat the water for doing the washing and for baths, which used to be taken in front of the kitchen fire in a portable, galvanised tub. On bath nights, the copper was filled from the well and lit. The tub was brought into the kitchen and the hot water put in from the copper. Afterwards, the water had to be carried away and tipped outside, so different from today, when you turn on taps and pull the plug when you've finished. It was quite understandable why some people did not have baths very often in those days. Lighting was either by candles or oil lamps, the latter having to be trimmed and filled every day. In spite of this, most of the cottages were kept spotlessly clean. It must have been a hard life for a young woman with several children.

On the outlying farms, shopping was restricted to the occasional trip to the local market town. Most villages had a bus service about twice a week, on market day and Saturday. The local butcher called on most houses at least once a week, the baker twice or three times weekly and the grocer used to visit, on a bicycle, once a fortnight to take the orders, which would be delivered a couple of days later. Food was cheap, but it needed to be when a family had to be brought up on less than two pounds a week, with no child allowance or social security to help. How people managed is still a mystery to me. I think they existed rather than lived, there being very little money left after the necessities of life had been purchased, and yet they had a fierce independence and hated charity of any kind. To apply for parish relief was considered such a disgrace as to be almost a crime. In my home village, several charities had been endowed to render assistance to villagers who were in need. For years, Father was a trustee and on many occasions he had great difficulty in persuading people (who through no fault of their own found themselves in trouble) that there was no disgrace in accepting help from one of the village charities.

The cottage gardens played a very important part in the feeding of the family. If a cottage did not have a large garden of about a quarter of an acre, no good farmworker would entertain living in it, because the vegetables were a major factor in feeding his family. Old Frank Parker used to reckon that a brace of rabbits a week and the garden would half keep you.

In spite of their undoubted hardships, or perhaps because of them, the older generation of farmworker had a great pride in his craft and in the farm he worked on. It was interesting to notice how the best farmers generally finished up with the best men. A good farmer would not keep a second-rate man for long and vice versa – a top class man not staying with a mediocre farmer. These men often put their job before anything else. Sammy Strange, one of the local farmers, used to tell a wonderful story about his shepherd. During the Depression, feedstuff, like everything else, became very cheap and Sammy bought a quantity of flake maize. On his rounds one morning, he told his shepherd what he had done and suggested that it would be a good idea to feed it to the lambs that were being fattened for market. The old shepherd was very non-committal. "Don't know about that. Might upset they lambs. Don't trust that foreign tackle." Now Sammy, being a sensible farmer, did not press the point, but sent up a couple of bags with the next lot of sheep corn. A few days later, Shep asked for some more corn to be sent up and added: "Thee cans't send on another couple o' bags o' that foreign tackle."

"I thought you said it wasn't any good and might upset the lambs. What changed your mind?" enquired Sammy.

"Well," replied Shep, "the dog ate some – didn't hurt she; then they kids ate it for two or three days and 'tain't hurt they yet, so I reckon it won't hurt the lambs."

Of the older generation of farmworker, I can only speak with admiration and respect. Masters of their craft, they educated me in their different skills. Harry Walbridge and Frank Parker showed me the intricate skills of hedge laying and rick making; and what Bill Hutchings did not know or could not do with horses was not worth knowing. Uncle Bert was cast in the same mould with dairy cattle and Percy Warren (of whom more later) instilled a great love of sheep that has remained with me all my life. There was no finesse about their method of instruction. They told you, they showed you and unless you did what you had been told, you received a good dressing-down. They were tough, hard taskmasters, but you could not argue with men who could do the job better and quicker than yourself.

The Hurdled Flock and Shepherds

THE last fifty years have brought great changes in agricultural practices, especially in the lowlands. None is more dramatic than the total disappearance of the hurdled sheep flocks of the south of England and the four-course arable rotation of which they were an integral part. This method of arable farming had held pride of place for over a hundred years on the chalk downland that stretches across the southern counties from Dorset to Kent. Before the advent of artificial manures and sprays, it was the only way that corn could be successfully grown on this thin chalkland.

The sheep flocks grazed the steep, unploughable slopes of the downs by day, returning to the arable land in the evening where they were folded over a succession of root and forage crops; they left behind a dressing of manure which, when ploughed in, provided the fertility for the ensuing grain crop. They also trod and compacted the soil, hence the two sayings "the golden hoof" and "the walking dung cart". In practice this meant that only about half the arable acreage of a farm was under corn each year, the rest being used to grow forage crops for the flock.

The actual folding entailed giving the sheep access to a fresh patch of food every day and was achieved by using temporary fencing which was moved forward daily. The two different types of fence used were sheep netting and hurdles. The sheep netting came in rolls fifty yards long, three feet six inches high with three-inch hexagon mesh.

This was erected on small posts known as shores or sales, which were cut out from hazel or ash saplings. They were two or three inches of diameter and about five feet long and were sharpened at one end. The hurdles were of two types: the wattle hurdle made from split hazel which grew in profusion in the coppices of Dorset, Wiltshire and Hampshire; and the gate hurdles of Sussex which were made from cleft ash, again plentiful in that part of the country.

The forage crops varied from farm to farm but were basically very similar. Swedes and kale were grown to be fed from December to the end of March, followed by rye, clover, trefoil and vetches until July; then came rape and turnips to last until the swedes became available again in December. Over the years, this system produced the Down breeds of today and also a breed of men who were unique in the agricultural industry. The first of the Down breeds to emerge was the Southdown, bred in the late eighteenth century at Glynde in Sussex by John Ellman, who improved the native heath sheep of that area. They were used extensively on the many native breeds across the southern and eastern part of the country and were directly responsible for the present-day Hampshire Down, Dorset Down, Shropshire Down, Suffolk and, indirectly, the Oxford Down. All these breeds were short-woolled, dense-fleeced sheep, very compact and heavily fleshed, extremely docile and easy to handle. It is interesting to note that when John Ellman dispersed his flock on his retirement in 1829, the one thousand four hundred head sold realised £78,624.75.

The shepherds who looked after these sheep were a law unto themselves in many cases, passing down their knowledge from generation to generation. They jealously guarded their knowledge from outsiders, keeping it very much a trade secret. In any case, in those days vets were never called in to treat sheep. There were no antibiotics or vaccines available; shepherds had to rely on the simple drugs and herbs, the secrets of which had been passed down from father to son for years. I use many of these old remedies even today and they are still very effective.

A head shepherd was a very important person in those days, taking orders from no one except the governor – and very few from him. Besides the actual shepherding, they had to move a lot of wire and hurdles every day and re-erect them. This meant a great deal of hard, physical work which they took a great pride in doing and doing well. The hurdles and wire were always erected in dead straight lines, with no odd hurdles or shores left behind the corn troughs and hay cribs, which were also moved forward daily. The needs of the flock were paramount as far as the shepherds were concerned and they were very dictatorial in this respect. They demanded, and got, whatever they asked for, without a thought as to whether or not it was convenient. If at lambing they required, say, a load of hay and some help, the boss would be told on his morning rounds: "I want a load of hay and a couple of hands to help I turn out they ewes and lambs; and get 'em up here reckly after breakfast."

Such an attitude may seem a little strange, but these men, with little or no formal education and no professional veterinary help, took full responsibility for a large flock of valuable sheep. The flock masters found the sheep and food and left the complete management of the flock to the shepherd, who put its well-being before anything and everything else, including himself. They were good shepherds, not because it paid them to be, but because it never entered their heads to be anything else.

The shepherd's hut was an essential part of the hurdled flock. About twelve feet long by six wide and mounted on four cast iron wheels, it was moved across the field behind the sheep. It was constructed mainly of corrugated iron and was lined inside with match-boarding. It contained a small coal-burning stove in one corner and, across the far end, a bunk with a cupboard fixed above. This contained the simple medicines, marking irons and paint which were in daily use. There was a line of nails behind the stable-type doors on which to hang coats and that made up the sum total of the furniture and fittings. The hut was generally half full of bags of feedstuff and the smell of linseed cake, Stockholm tar and wet coats filled the air. This was where the shepherd ate his meals, kept his tools and sheltered from the weather. It was also his home for a month or six weeks at lambing time. The hurdled flocks were always lambed where the fodder was growing, so it was rare for the lambing yard to be near the shepherd's home, which meant that he lived in the hut during January and February. The lambing yards were sited in a different place each year to avoid the danger of infectious disease carrying over from one lambing to the next.

The yards were constructed of hurdles thatched with wheat straw; a square fold was pitched out allowing two or three sheep per hurdle square. Around the inside of the fold coops were made, small pens one hurdle square with a thatched roof lean-to, into which the newly born lambs were placed with their mothers. The centre of the fold, which was really an open yard, was bedded up daily with straw and this was where the in-lamb ewes stayed during the night. During the day they were turned out to feed and, as each of them lambed, they were put into individual coops for a couple of days before being moved into a nursery pen where they stayed until the lambs were strong enough to be turned on to the fold, only being brought in if the weather was bad. This was where, for a month or more, the shepherds worked, ate and slept, being shepherd, midwife and doctor rolled into one.

Alas, they are no more. Their Down ewes have been superseded by crossbred grass sheep, brought in mainly from Scotland and Wales to produce lambs for slaughter. Gone are the days of the self-contained pure-bred flocks where the shepherds could, and did, derive pride and satisfaction from breeding their own replacements and improving their flocks. Nowadays, both the ewes and the rams are bought in and the shepherd has become a shepherd no more – merely a mass producer of lambs. Those solid, dignified shepherds of my youth with their bob-tailed sheep dogs and their crooks have disappeared and the countryside is a poorer place for their passing.

It was into this world of pedigree hurdled ram breeding sheep and their shepherds that I found myself in the latter part of the 1950s. Since leaving school I had been with my uncle on a family farm in Dorset and, as was the way in those days in this part of the world, we learned to do every job on the farm and do it well. Uncle Bert's maxim was that you never expected anyone to do what you were not prepared to do yourself and if you took the hardest job you could set the pace. By the time I had reached my mid-twenties I had mastered the art of rick making, thatching, hedging, had driven horses and tractors and worked with the dairy herd.

I had also developed a great affection for sheep. The person responsible for this interest was a neighbouring farmer, Percy Warren, who kept a flock of Dorset Horns which he shepherded himself. A thickset, grey-haired man in his fifties, he was typical of the working farmer of the time, putting the stock and the farm's needs before his own personal comfort or pleasure. As a young man, I spent a lot of summer evenings in his company, listening to him expound the art and mystery of shepherding. The ideas he instilled into me some fifty years ago still remain to this day, as do so many of the old remedies which he had learned from his father and which, in turn, he passed on to me. Sheep and shepherding are things you either love or hate and they are a love that has remained with me since those days.

In September 1951 I was married to Dorothy, whose father farmed nearby, and, thinking back to that time, it seems almost impossible to realise what a state the country was in. Six years had passed since we had won the Second World War and yet food, sweets and petrol were still rationed, as were clothes; and we had to apply for coupons to be able to purchase furniture. In spite of all these restrictions, life went on, although it was a very austere existence. We had two sons, David, born in 1952, and Russell, in 1955.

For several years after our marriage we moved around the country, working with commercial sheep most of the time; then in 1957 I had the chance to take a pedigree ram breeding flock and we went to live in Somerset.

The Vale Country

THE first flock of Dorset Downs that I took on was at Halse, in Taunton Vale, some eight miles west of Taunton with the Brendon Hills to the north-west and the Quantocks to the north-east. The lower half of the farm was on very heavy clay that in winter stuck to your boots like glue, in contrast to the top side, which consisted of a red loam. This vale country differed from the chalk downs in many ways: apart from the difference in soil, the fields tended to be much smaller, with high banked hedges and a ditch either side. The hedge banks themselves also contained many trees. The farm was about two-thirds arable; it was reasonably flat and intersected by several lanes.

The flock consisted of around two hundred and fifty breeding ewes, plus ewe hogs. Some one hundred rams were sold annually. The flock was run in the traditional way, except that the hurdles used were made of one-and-a-half inch by quarter-inch bar iron, and instead of wooden and wire shores, iron stakes were used. These consisted of a length of half-inch round bar split at the top for about an inch and opened out to form a "Y" at the top. A leg was welded on at right angles about a foot from the bottom to form a shape like the letter "H". The wire was run out, then the leg placed over the bottom strand and pushed down into the ground with a foot; then the wire was pulled up and the top strand placed into the "Y" at the top of the stake, the leg holding the bottom down and the "Y" the top up. These stakes were quick and very effective when used in clay or loam but difficult, if not impossible, on stony land.

I had taken on the flock from Joe Thorne, a shepherd who had worked on the farm for over fifty years and had received his Royal Society long-service medal from the Queen Mother. He was a grand old chap who still did odd jobs round the farm when he was over seventy. In his youth he had learned to shear with the blades using both right and left hands. With his right hand he would open up the belly and both back legs, then up the neck from the shoulder to the ears, working around the breast until he had cleaned out the neck back to the shoulder. Next, with the sheep still sitting up on its bottom, he would push her head between his legs and shear off her near-side from shoulder to tail as far around as the backbone. He would then step around the sheep, with her head still between his legs, and, using his left hand all the time, would shear her off-side in the same manner, taking little narrow blows never more than an inch wide, running up from the belly to meet at the backbone in a herringbone pattern. He had learned this method as a young man when a flock of Devon longwools had been kept on the farm, and he could remember when a team of oxen had been used for plough-ing the heavy land.

It was at this time that I met two of the great Dorset Down shepherds of the day: Dennis Buckingham and Frank Radford. Both were unique in my experience and they would give help and advice if asked. They were both very successful shepherds, keen rivals and great friends. On their own, both had a great wealth of knowledge and experience in shepherding; together they were well-nigh invincible in sheep matters. They used to regularly do what I have never seen anyone else attempt. On the show field, the day before judging, they used to trim together. Dennis would hold the sheep by a halter and trim the head, neck and shoulders back to the middle ribs; Frank, meanwhile, would trim the back, back end and flanks and no one could see where they met. They used to trim one complete string and then the other – twenty-four sheep in all. After stopping for dinner and a few bottles of brown ale they used to speed up dramatically!

Dennis had a great way with dogs. I never knew him have a proper collie, but generally a crossbreed of some sort that he had been given. The one that springs to mind in particular was a long-coated, black and tan dog who answered to the name of "Bonzo". He looked like a cross between a Devon-type collie and an Old English bob-tail with a bit of something else for luck. If Dennis wished to catch a sheep he could do so anywhere: Bonzo could hold them together in a corner, on a straight hedge, or in the middle of a field. When moving sheep along the road, Dennis would ride his bicycle slowly in front and Bonzo brought the sheep along behind. In the summer, the ewes used to run on some steep fields on the other side of a narrow valley from where his trimming shed was situated. Dennis would come out, look across to the ewes on the opposite side of the valley and, if one was cast on her back, he would shout: "Bonzo, ewe on her back." Bonzo would come tearing out from the shed where he had been asleep in the straw. "Arf arf-ing" as he came down across the field, over the little stream and up into the steep or sideling field where the ewes were, he'd stop, look around until he spotted the cast ewe and with a renewed "Arf, arf" he'd tear off once again up to the sheep, grab a front leg in his mouth and pull her over downhill. Then, at the same mad speed, he would return to the trimming shed, yapping all the way. If you heard Bonzo in full cry you knew that Dennis had a sheep on her back.

Dennis really excelled at trimming and could trim sheep to perfection at great speed. As a young man I used to marvel at the way he went about it, bits of wool flying in all directions from a pair of shears that cut like a razor. I envied his skill and the apparent ease with which he could transform a perfectly ordinary-looking sheep into something really smart, in a very short time. On one occasion he had sold out at Exeter market with the exception of one ram which had a woolly face and loose coat. He offered it for twenty guineas to a customer who refused it. He took it back the next week after plucking the face and tightening the coat; the same customer bought him for twenty-seven guineas!

The year the Royal Counties was at Portsmouth he had a wonderful shearling ewe out: she won the Devon County, Bath and West, Royal Counties and the Royal. As at most shows, parties of schoolchildren used to visit on the third day. After breakfast, Dick Knight and I were sitting on the hurdles next to Dennis's ewe – he had gone off to watch the sheep shearing competition. While we were sitting there a party of about twenty schoolboys came round. Now this ewe, in spite of having been out several times, was very nervous – or as we would describe her, sharp. She was in a corner pen and unfortunately the pen behind her was empty. The kids went up to the front of her pen and off she shot to the back. A couple of boys got into the empty pen and they had her going back and forth across the pen like a bat out of hell. Dick had a diplomatic word with the offenders: "I should stop that if I were you, sonny. Now come on out of that pen."

One of the lads looked up with a cheeky grin on his face. "I ain't doing no harm guv'nor. I ain't even touched her." And with this he gave the hurdle a kick and off across the pen she went again.

At that moment Dennis came wandering back, turning the corner as his beloved ewe shot across her pen. He was an obsessive snuff taker and was in the act of taking a pinch when everything happened at once. "You little buggers," he roared. With that, the boys scattered, frightening the ewe even more so that she jumped at the hurdles and got stuck half way over. The snuff box went flying through the air to land in the straw of the next pen. Dennis grabbed his ewe and lifted her back into the pen, then gave Dick and me a good dressing-down for not stopping the boys sooner. When we suggested that it was his shouting that had frightened the ewe most, we got a proper cussing and spent the next half-hour looking for the snuff box in the straw.

This snuff box came in useful on another occasion. We were all sleeping in the accommodation provided on the ends of the lines and in the adjoining pen was a bad-tempered Wiltshire Horn ram. If anyone went up to his pen he would back off and then charge at the hurdles. The night before judging he kept banging away at the hurdles, keeping everyone awake. The next evening we had all been out for a drink and returned for supper before turning in. As he passed the ram's pen, Dennis absent-mindedly put his hand on the top rail of the hurdle. The ram charged. Dennis sensed him coming and pulled his hand away just in time.

"We got to do something about these tool before he does some damage," he exclaimed. "Now, two of ee get one each side of I, then I'll toll him up again and when he hits the hurdle you grab a horn each." We took up position, Dennis banged the hurdle with his hat and, true to form, the ram had another go, banging his head into the top of the hurdles once again. As he did so, two of us grabbed a horn each and hung on for grim death. Under Dennis's instructions we dragged him forward until his nose was sticking out over the top of the hurdle. Meanwhile, Dennis had fished out his snuff box from the top pocket of his long-sleeved corduroy waistcoat. He shook out quite a little heap of snuff into the palm of his hand and with a cautionary "You two hold on like hell", slapped his hand around the ram's nose and held it there until the snuff had been inhaled. "Alright, let him go," he ordered. We complied and got our hands out of the way double quick, but there was no need. Instead of coming for us the ram backed off, coughing, sneezing and farting in quick succession with tears running down his face. We had a peaceful night, with no banging of hurdles to keep us awake. Next morning, he looked as though he had a hangover and was quite subdued for the rest of the show.

The following evening we went to a neighbouring public house. We were sitting in the bar having a quiet drink when two of the regulars, who were playing about on the dartboard, approached our party and enquired if anyone fancied a game. Dennis and Arthur (Head Shepherd at Newburgh) accepted and suggested the best two of three games for half-pints. The local spokesman intimated that they only played for pints, to which Arthur replied: "So be it." I believe those locals thought they were on to a good thing – and events proved that they could play darts quite well – but they had no idea what they were letting themselves in for. Dennis was quite a formidable opponent, but Arthur was in a class of his own. He played darts the way he did everything else, slowly, methodically and with unshakeable confidence. He would hold a dart at arm's length, slowly bring it back almost up to his eye, then fling it with deadly accuracy and great force. After Arthur and Dennis had won three pints without losing a single game, the locals decided enough was enough and remembered pressing engagements elsewhere.

Frank Radford was another of the old school and a great judge of sheep; he had that great ability to spot the maker. A short, thickset man with a ready smile and a jocular nature, he had had quite an adventurous youth. As a teenager he had a row with the farm bailiff, tipping him off his horse and, being afraid to go back home, had walked the eight miles into Taunton, joined the Somerset Light Infantry and served the next four years in India before returning home.

My one sad recollection of Halse concerned Tiger Millett. There was a large manor house in the village that had been converted for use as an old people's home and it was to here that Bill came. I had not seen him for nearly twenty years and it was difficult to imagine that this tiny, shrunken man was the same person for whom, as a boy, I had blown the forge, watched in admiration as he shod awkward horses and listened enthralled to his tales of army life in India. He had never married, but lived with his mother until her death and then with his elder brother and his wife, until they passed away. He had no other close relatives and was all alone in his old age. He died a few months later and, as he wished, now rests in the church-yard at Beckington.

One night I had the closest shave of my life, when we were out rabbiting with the Land Rover. The governor and the foreman were in the back; they had folded the canvas tilt back and were standing between the middle and back tubular supports. On the way across a stubble field I picked up a rabbit in the headlights and off we went in pursuit. Just as the governor put up his gun, I hit a combine rut and his feet slipped out from under him, bringing the gun down. There was an almighty bang and the windscreen fell out. I thought that the shot had ricocheted back, so stopped and turned off the engine. The governor came running round to me. "You all right, Shep? You all right?"

"I'm alright, but look at the windscreen," I replied. Then I felt something warm and sticky running down my neck, put a hand up and found it covered in blood. I turned round and found a hole in the cab big enough to put a fist through. The shot had blown a hole in the cab, grazed the top of my head and blown out the windscreen. Back to the farm we went, all in rather a state of shock and had a stiff Scotch. They washed the blood away and it did not look too bad, but the next day I had to go to hospital and they removed nine pellets from the top of my head, giving me a Yul Brynner haircut to do so. I don't believe in taking too many chances and have never been out shooting at night since.

It was shortly after coming to Halse and getting onto the show circuit that I joined the British Herdsmen's Club, an association to which practically all the professional stockmen belonged at that time. The Club had been founded at a meeting of herdsmen held at the Birmingham Farm Stock Show on December 1st, 1894. The original resolution moved read as follows:

> That the Herdsmen attending the Birmingham and London Smithfield Shows form a club, which shall hold a meeting annually in London at Smithfield time, each member of such Club shall pay a small annual subscription in order to provide prizes for the Herdsmen in charge of animals gaining the Champion male and female prizes at the London Show.

The membership of the Club, which was first known as "The Herdsmen's Smithfield Club", was not large, being restricted to members who exhibited at Smithfield. The subscriptions were small and the bulk of its funds was derived from donations generously given by breeders and others who were interested both in its workings and in the herdsmen. At the turn of the century, the Club expanded its membership to include shepherds, pigmen and horsemen, adopting the name "The British Herdsmen's Club" and with the following objectives:

> Improving and maintaining the comfort and welfare of stockmen, especially at Agricultural Shows, and to render assistance to Members in need of help.

In the early 1960s, as the number of showmen began to decrease and membership to fall, various local branches were formed on a county basis which many commercial dairymen and shepherds joined. The Clubs ran monthly meetings during the winter, with speakers giving talks ranging from feeding dairy cows to bee-keeping, and farm walks were arranged during the summer. Funds were raised by a series of dances, whist drives and bingo evenings, the highlight of the year being the Annual Dinner.

The first local branch was formed in Dorset at the instigation of the then National Chairman, Fred Thorne, ably assisted by Larry Gee, who for many years acted as Secretary. Some eight or ten branches were formed during the sixties and seventies but, sadly, several failed to succeed, the great decrease in the labour force employed by the industry being the chief reason. The dairy industry was the prime example, for in the 1960s the ratio of cows to a man would have been thirty or forty; now it is more like one hundred and twenty. The same applies to sheep; two to three hundred ewes per shepherd has now become six hundred to a thousand. It is against this greatly decreased membership that we have struggled during the last fifteen years, but we still survive with a hard core of members and several very enthusiastic branches, thanks in many ways to our Secretary, Bernard Mulvaney, who for the last twenty-five years has worked continuously for the Club's welfare and survival.

The branches hold an Any Questions session and dinner during the winter and a National Herdsman of the Year competition, together with the Annual General Meeting in the summer. At the Royal we have a marquee where members can get a cup of tea and a sandwich, sit down and have a chat or watch television. It has become a very popular focal point for members, especially during the evenings. For the past twenty-two years, Dorothy has run the tent, which has entailed a lot of hard work on her part.

The Club also provides liaison officers at the Royal Show and in 1994 we celebrated the Club's centenary with a luncheon at which the principal speaker was the Chairman of the Royal Smithfield Club. In this centenary year I had the honor to be the Club's Chairman.

Newburgh

IN the 1960s Newburgh was a typical Dorset downland farm, extending to over a thousand acres. Like so many large farms in the area it was long and narrow, stretching from the water meadows at the bottom end up to the ridge of the down at the top – a distance of some three miles. The main road from Dorchester to Wool cut through the lower part of the farm, with some hundred acres, mostly water meadows, on the north side of the road extending right down to the river and Winfrith Heath. This land consisted of a very light, dark soil almost like peat. To the south of the main road there was a band of good, deep, heavy loam over the chalk, extending for half a mile as the land rose towards the ridge. The soil gradually got thinner until it was right on the chalk. The last couple of hundred acres, right on the top, had a clay cap over the chalk. The farmer, William Hooper, used to maintain that if there were seven different types of soil in Dorset, he had eight at Newburgh.

Like so many farms in the area, Newburgh had been, up to the Depression of the twenties and thirties, primarily arable, carrying a hurdled flock of over six hundred Dorset Down ewes with two hundred ewe tegs (ewes under two years old retained for flock replacement). There was just one dairy being milked on the water meadows to the north side of the main road. By the sixties there were three dairies containing nearly two hundred cows, with all the heifer calves being reared for replacement and sale. The

Dorset Down flock had been reduced to three hundred ewes and a hundred ewe tegs. Some four hundred acres of corn was grown annually, all spring barley, much of which went for malting. A road ran due south from the main road up through the middle of the farm, coming out at the top end on the Wool to Lulworth road. The farmhouse, five cottages and the main buildings were situated on this road, about half a mile from the main road. One dairy was milked here, another on the water meadows below the road and a third right at the top of the farm, almost up to the Lulworth road at Belhuish. There was another set of buildings and a stockman's cottage half way up the farm between the home buildings and Belhuish.

Including the gardener, lorry driver and maintenance man, some twenty men were employed full time, eight of whom had worked on the farm, for the same family, for over forty years.

Mr William, or the Governor as he was always called (but invariably referred to affectionately behind his back as Billy Boss), was a typical yeoman farmer. At that time he and his two brothers were farming some four-and-a-half thousand acres in Dorset. Just after the First World War his father and uncle had four hurdled flocks of Down sheep totalling over two thousand ewes. Billy Boss was a rather short, thickset man with a round face and a ready smile – and in contrast to the popular belief that farmers are usually overbearing, he was a quiet, gentle-mannered man.

Every morning he was out by six-thirty, walking up to the home dairy to see the head dairyman. At about ten to seven he met the foreman, discussed the day's work with him for a few minutes and left to give the tractor drivers and labourers their orders. Then, getting into his Land Rover, he drove off to the bottom dairy; after seeing that all was well he drove right up to the other end of the farm to see the dairyman at the top dairy. After that, he visited all the tractor drivers and labourers to see them started at work and finally arrived at the sheep fold where he generally spent about fifteen minutes discussing the flock's health and requirements. Then it was back for his breakfast at about nine o'clock, by which time he had visited all three dairies, been from one end of the farm to the other, seen all the men started at their work and finally met the shepherds. I once asked him how big a farm it was possible to run efficiently. His reply was: "No bigger than you can get round properly before breakfast every day."

Billy Boss had started farming in his own right in the depths of the agricultural depression in the late 1920s, taking the tenancy of an entirely arable farm. He told me the only grass field was seven acres where the cart horses used to run at night during the summer. At that time he reckoned it was impossible to grow corn on chalk arable and make a profit. He sowed down part of the farm to permanent grass and installed a dairy herd, and when he could not find a market for his milk he made it into butter and sold it locally. He established a flock of Dorset Horn sheep and over the years these became one of the leading flocks of the breed. In the 1950s his uncle, Tom Hooper, retired and Billy Boss moved to Newburgh; in so doing, he took over his uncle's flock of Dorset Downs, established in 1872 by his grandfather. The Newburgh sheep were renowned for being one of the top flocks of Dorset Downs in the country.

This was the man I went to work for as head shepherd in the early 1960s, and he taught me more about the finer points of sheep, shepherding and farming than anyone else before or since. He was a man of immense patience who would always explain the reasons behind his decisions and ideas, but he was always ready to listen to suggestions or points of view. He also had a great knack of quietly keeping your feet on the ground when things were going well and cheering you up and helping you on when they were going wrong. If you had problems with the job, as long as you were trying your hardest to put them right, he never grumbled or complained.

Arthur Whittle had spent his entire working life with the Newburgh flock, starting as shepherd's boy at thirteen years old, then under shepherd and finally head shepherd, a post he held for over thirty years. He was a big, somewhat ponderous man, a shepherd of the old school who put the well-being of his sheep before everything and everybody, including himself. For most of his life he had worked for Tom Hooper, who had been a very successful farmer and flock master; according to Arthur, things had never been the same since Mr Tom retired and never would be again. At times Arthur led Billy Boss a proper dance. His favourite way of closing an argument was: "If Mr Tom were here he would never do it, but then he were a proper farmer."

Unless he had visitors or we were sorting sheep, it was very rare for Billy Boss to come round again after his morning visit, but one spring, for some reason, he started to pay us a second visit in the late afternoon. After this had gone on for several days, Arthur began to get a little peevish about these afternoon calls, and when Billy Boss asked him how things were, he got the reply: "None the better for your asking."

"Oh, and what have I done wrong now?" Billy enquired.

"I'll tell thee," said Arthur, "When a farmer sees his sheep and shepherd every morning afore breakfast, that be not only good farming but also good manners, but when he do come twice a day that be damn bad manners."

The afternoon visits ceased.

Arthur was getting towards his mid-sixties and wanted to take things easier, especially showing, which meant staying away from home for several nights at a time, so it was decided that I should become head man and Arthur would stay on as under shepherd. Actually it never worked out like that at all. How the devil could it? Arthur was old enough to be my father and had been with the flock all his working life, and for the last twenty-odd years he had been in charge. He also knew how to handle the governor. How could I, a newcomer, tell him what to do? I am pleased to say that I had more sense than to try. We got on wonderfully well and never had a serious disagreement all the time we were working together – and within a year we had the flock back in the prize money, just as it had been in Mr Tom's heyday. This pleased Arthur immensely and although he never came out to shows to stay, he generally turned up for the judging; and he could still show a sheep with anyone when he put his mind to it.

Our first Champion was at the Royal Counties and, as was customary, Billy Boss took all the flock masters and shepherds to the refreshment tent for a celebration drink. Bobby Mitchell, a grand old shepherd from Sussex, who was always in the prize money, congratulated Mr William on winning and, turning to Arthur, remarked: "What's on then, ain't had no trouble with you lately?" Arthur (who by this time had drunk a few) drained his glass and, smiling all over his face, replied: "No, but thee's likely to get a lot more."

Arthur never took the same interest in ram selling as I did. His over-riding love was breeding females. I once asked him what his greatest ambition was. He answered without hesitation: "To breed the finest flock of ewes in the country." This was one of the great lessons he taught me. You have got to be able to breed females before you can breed rams.

The flock was run in the traditional way. Three hundred

breeding ewes were kept in regular ages. All the ewes were sold as regular draft (five years old) after having had three crops of lambs. One hundred and fifty of the best ewe lambs were retained for flock replacements and sale each year. The top hundred went into the flock to replace the regular draft ewes which had been sold, and the remaining fifty were sold as two teeth. Just over one hundred ram lambs were kept for sale as stud rams and the remainder of the lamb crop was sold as milk lambs, mostly in time for the Easter market.

The flock was hurdled all year round with wire netting and wattle hurdles, of which we had some forty dozen. Arthur was a craftsman at pitching these. I don't think he could have put them up crooked if he had tried. Lambing took place in December and we used to erect a lambing yard with hurdles at a different site each year. I had been used to putting up lambing pens for years – pens that I had always thought quite adequate – but Arthur's idea of a lambing yard was quite palatial. First, the actual yard where the in-lamb ewes were to lie was pitched out twelve hurdles square. The inside of this yard was lined with pens or coops each a hurdle square, where the newly born lambs were penned with their mothers. These pens were covered with a sloping roof of thatched hurdles so that there was an open yard with some forty-odd cubicles all round the outside, all of which were roofed over. A gateway two hurdles wide was left on one side as an entrance. A smaller gateway in the opposite side led to the nursery pens. These were really a continuation of the main yard and were the same width and the same eight hurdles long with a thatched roof on three sides. This pen was divided into two: one half for ewes with twin lambs, the other for ewes with singles. A fold twelve hurdles square was pitched outside the entrance. This was where the ewes were fed their hay. Finally, the shepherd hut was pulled into place alongside the entrance with a window looking out over the lambing yard.

We had an extremely good hut at Newburgh, lined inside with match-boarding, a built-in bunk at the front and a round, cast iron stove behind the door at the other end. It had been on the farm as long as Arthur could remember. Carved into the match-boarding over the bunk were the names of the shepherds who had tended the flock over the years, including the great pre-war shepherd, Tommy Wiltshire. The inscription that intrigued me most read: "Shep Fox, head man on this place for thirty-seven years, 1931." According to Arthur, he had been an autocratic man who ruled the sheep and everyone including the governor. (Arthur must have been his star pupil!) At that time, the flock consisted of six hundred ewes and two hundred and fifty tegs. Towards the end of his career old Shep Fox was crippled with rheumatism and had great difficulty in getting about, so he was fitted up with a donkey and cart. Every morning he drove up to the fold, unharnessed the donkey and turned it into the fold with the ewes, where it stayed feeding until it was time to go home. The sheep took no notice of it at all.

We put the ewes into the lambing yard by night for about a week prior to lambing. When they started, I did the night and early morning stints. Arthur arrived at the fold at seven o'clock, at which time we filled the ash hay cribs in the outside pens – two dozen hay cribs for the three hundred ewes. While they were eating their hay, the ewes that had already lambed were fed with turnips, hay and cake. These ewes would either be in the cubicle pen or in the nursery pens. Just before breakfast, the in-lamb ewes were driven out to their fold of grass and given their cake so that, by nine o'clock, all the sheep had been seen to and fed. After breakfast, the lambs which had been born in the previous twenty-four hours were tattooed with an individual number in their ear and ear-nipped to denote their sire, with a further nip in the top of the left ear for twins. It was then possible to tell at a glance if the sheep was a twin or single and by whom it had been sired.

After being ear-nipped and tattooed, the lambs which were strong enough were moved from the cubicles into the nursery pens. Singles were moved at a day old (or two at the most). Twins were very often kept in individual pens for three or four days. When in the nursery, the couples (ewe with her lamb or lambs) were allowed to run out onto the grass by day and after about a week were kept out altogether and folded over the grass daily, with the lambs running into a front fold through a creep hurdle. These hurdles were made with a series of upright rollers spaced about nine inches apart, through which the lambs could easily pass but which were too narrow to allow the ewes to get through.

Directly after dinner, or just before if the weather was really bad, the in-lamb ewes were brought back into the lambing yard and given another feed of hay. Any ewes that showed signs of uneasiness before breakfast were kept back, so the number of lambs born outside during the morning used to be very small. The couples were fed again and shut into the nursery pens, and at about four o'clock the in-lamb ewes were all driven from the hay pen into the lambing yard for the night.

The night work consisted of inspecting the sheep at regular intervals, putting into cubicles those which had lambed, giving assistance when required and making sure that the newly born lambs were being mothered and suckling. It also involved keeping an eye on the nursery pens to see that all was well. These days, lowland sheep are lambed in permanent buildings with water and electric light, which makes things much more comfortable, especially for the shepherds. But I often look back with nostalgia to those days and nights lambing a flock on the top of the downs – coming out of the sheep house in the early hours of the morning with a Tilley lantern and standing by the yard entrance before going in. The deep murmur of a ewe answered by the feeble bleat of a lamb she had just dropped would tell you that there was a fresh addition to the flock. Or there would be the groan of a ewe in labour that might require help and, as you slowly made your way around the yard, stepping over the ewes lying in their bed of straw, you spotted her stretched out on her side heaving away. Hanging the lantern on the nearest hurdle you quietly examined her. If the two feet and nose were in place, you helped the lamb away and put mother and baby into a pen.

Sometimes complications occurred: a head or legs could be back, or twins could be coming together. You then penned the ewe, fetched some warm water from the kettle in the sheep house, took off your coat, soaped up and got on with the job of acting midwife. Half an hour later, with the ewe safely lambed and the lambs suckling, you returned to the sheep house for a cup of tea, congratulated yourself on a job well done, then took one last look round before catching a few hours' sleep.

Lambing is, without a doubt, the busiest time of year for a shepherd, both in terms of hours worked and mental strain. It can also be a time of great satisfaction and sense of achievement. First of all there is the miracle of reproduction: to find three live animals where but a few minutes before there had only been one is something that never fails to thrill me. The deep mutter of the ewe as she licks and cleans her newborn lamb, the lamb struggling to its feet when a few minutes old and staggering round its mother's side looking for her teats, being gently assisted with a nudge and push from her nose until it manages to get the teat into its mouth, followed by the gentle slumping as it sucks away with its little tail waggling, is indeed a wonderful sight.

Looking round an hour later to see the lamb clean and dry, its tummy full of milk, lying by its mother's side on the clean straw, never ceases to impress me with the wonders of nature. You forget the long hours, the cold, wet days and nights with the disappointments, occasional disasters and tragedies that always occur some time during lambing. It is wonderful to see the baby lambs asleep with their mothers and the in-lamb ewes lying down chewing their cud and, with a glance up at the starlit night sky, you realise at that moment that God's in his heaven and all's right with the world.

Lambing was generally over by mid-January and towards the end of the month the ewes and lambs were moved into kale and swedes, which lasted them until mid-April. This was a period of hard, monotonous work, often carried out in cold, wet conditions. The flock would be divided into four groups: the ewes with single lambs in one; the ewes and twins in another; about twenty of the best lambs with their mothers in a third; and the ewe hoggets in the fourth.

They were folded across the roots, each flock having a fresh patch every day. The lambs were always folded in front of their mothers, which allowed them to pick off the best of the roots and to be fed corn without interference from the ewes. They were able to get back to their mothers through the creep hurdle. Every day, the hurdles and wire were carried forward through the kale and swedes, the covered lamb troughs and hay cribs moved on, and the fold set.

We used to reckon to corn the ewes, move on the lamb creep hurdles and covered troughs so that the lambs could go forward, put their corn in, let on the ewes and, with a bit of luck, carry most of the hurdles forward before breakfast, which we used to have about nine-thirty. After breakfast, the hurdles were pitched up in readiness for the next day. It was an unwritten law that we never had to pitch hurdles after mid-day dinner. We very often did, to get forward, but the next-day fold had to be in place in the morning and if for any reason it was not, there was hell to pay. By mid-afternoon the ewes would have eaten most of their roots and at about four o'clock their hay cribs were filled, the lambs corned again and they were left for the night.

Around mid-February, choosing a fine day, the lambs were tailed. This was a major operation. The day before, several ash faggots and quite a heap of leg wood (firewood) were brought up the the field. When the lambs were let forward, a hurdle was placed across the creeps to stop them going back with their mothers and a pen was erected in a corner of the fold into which they were driven in readiness for tailing. About nine o'clock, two of the farm workers, Bill Voicey and Bobby Burt, arrived and lit the fire and after breakfast we were ready to start.

The tailing irons were put in the fire to get hot and the tailing stool was placed at right angles to the pen of lambs. Arthur sat astride the stool, then Bobby handed him a lamb which he held by one front and one back leg in each hand. The lamb was placed on the stool with its back against Arthur's chest. I pulled its tail out straight along the stool and, taking a hot iron from the fire, removed the tail leaving a stump about two inches long. The combined cutting and cauterising action of the hot iron prevents any bleeding. As soon as the tail was off, Arthur put the lamb down on its feet and away it ran to its mother and started sucking, apparently not noticing that it had left its tail behind. As the lambs were tailed, the tails were put into two heaps: one for rams, the other for ewes.

The tailing of lambs may seem a rather barbaric practice

but it was, and still is, an essential part of lowland sheep husbandry. Unlike the hill sheep which are rarely tailed and feed, for the most part, off coarse, hard herbage and are stocked at up to 3 acres per sheep, our lowland sheep live off much more succulent and tender food and are stocked at 3 to 4 sheep to the acre. This means that their droppings are much softer; unless their tails are removed they would very quickly get messy around their back ends, which in turn would mean fly infestation and maggots.

We reckoned to finish by dinner time, having done some four hundred lambs. The two heaps of tails were counted and tied up into bundles of twenty and then, for the first time, we knew how many lambs we had. It was considered to be courting disaster to count up the lambs before tailing. In any case, the lambing bonus was only paid on the number of lambs tailed. Any that were lost between lambing and tailing were not paid for.

The tails were used to make a great West Country dish, delicious lamb tail pie. The shepherds had first pick (the biggest ones), then the governor had his and the remainder were taken down to the home building where the rest of the staff helped themselves. To those people who have never tasted lamb tail pie, I would suggest that they have missed one of the gastronomic delights of English cooking.

The kale and swedes were finished by early April and we then moved into rye with a few mangolds scattered around. About this time the lambs were weaned and put into two folds: one of ram lambs, the other ewe lambs. The folds were pitched big enough for sufficient grub to be left behind for the ewes to clear up overnight. By day they were turned out of the fold into the steep-sided valley at the top end of the farm, being driven up first thing every morning and brought back in the afternoon. This has been standard practice on downland arable farms for over a hundred years.

The rye lasted for only two or three weeks. By the end of April it runs up to spill (goes to seed) and loses its feeding value, so around the first week in May we moved into clover or trefoil for a month, by which time the vetches were fit. Shearing took place in May. The draft ewes and two teeth were always shorn the week before the Devon County Show, the four and six teeth ewes and the ewe lambs between the Devon County and the Bath and West. (The number of teeth indicates the age of the sheep: two teeth were two years old, four teeth were three years old and six teeth were four years old.)

At that time, almost everyone washed the sheep before shearing, because the wool from sheep that had been washed commanded a higher price. It also made shearing much easier, for the fleeces of ewes that had been folded on roots all winter, especially if it had been a wet time, were full of dried soil which played havoc with combs and cutters.

The wash at Newburgh was situated at the north end of the farm bordering on Winfrith Heath, where a stream ran through the water meadows on its way to the Frome. About thirty feet of the stream's banks had to be walled up so that, when the hatch was dropped, there was a channel of water four or five feet wide, six feet deep and some ten yards long with a sloping ramp at one end where the sheep could walk out. They were put in by the hatch and had to swim the length of the channel against the current. Four or five men were stationed at regular intervals along the channel with so-called wooden rubbers to keep the animals moving as they swam down the wash. Their fleeces spread out and we could see the dirt coming out, leaving a dirty brown cloud in the water behind them.

Washing meant an early start for us, as the sheep had to be penned beside the wash by six o'clock to start at seven. We were finished by breakfast-time and we then had to drive the flock back to the fold. This was generally a slow job, as the old ewes did not move very well when soaked with water.

Shearing took place in the big barn at the home building. Blades were used until 1917 at Newburgh, but in that year a Wolseley shearing machine was installed. This was still in use in the late 1960s – and still in immaculate condition. A beam over twenty feet long spanned the barn from wall to wall about eight feet from the floor. (This beam had been cut by a German prisoner of war in Coombe Wood, and squared and straightened with an adze.) A shafting ran the length of the beam with a fast-and-loose pulley at one end to take the drive. Fixed at regular intervals along the shaft were four bevelled pulleys which drove the machines. Two cords hung down from each machine. When the first was pulled it engaged a leather friction pulley on the machine with the bevelled pulley on the shaft, which in turn drove the cable and the hand piece. When the second cord was pulled, it disengaged the pulleys and the hand piece stopped. The outfit had originally been driven by a horizontal oil engine, but this had been replaced in the 1950s by an electric motor. The original hand pieces were still in use: narrow, three-fingered cutters and laced leather hand pieces. I helped shear with this outfit when it was fifty years old and it was as trouble-free and efficient as the day it was made – a great tribute to the engineers who designed and built it.

Several of the staff were excellent shearers. Slow, perhaps, by modern standards, but the sheep were beautifully turned out: legs shorn to the ground, faces and ears cleaned right out and not a blow mark showing. To nip a sheep was almost a crime, but to cut one brought Arthur down like a ton of bricks. As he dabbed turpentine on the cut, he would remind the shearer that he was in a shearing barn, not a slaughter house.

At shearing time, we always penned the ewes overnight at the back of the barn behind the machines. To keep them clean the barn had been bedded up with green stinging nettles. If straw were used it would stick onto the wool and be impossible to get out of the shorn fleece. This would, and still does, greatly devalue the wool. There were always three or four men shearing, with one bringing out the sheep and another tying the wool. In those days each fleece was rolled and tied separately before being put in the wool sheet. Gordon, the maintenance man, ground the combs and cutters, kept the machines oiled and, most important of all, made the tea, using his Calor gas blow-lamp to boil the kettle. In the days of the old water-cooled engine, the boiling water used to be drawn from the engine hopper. Arthur reckoned that at times the tea used to taste a bit oily!

We always used to age-mark the ewes: two teeth on the left shoulder, four teeth in the middle of the back, six teeth left pin, regular draft around the corner on the right pin. A day or two before shearing we used to go through the flock, part the wool and put a paint spat right down on the skin one place forward from where it was the year before, so as the sheep walked off the shearing floor they were carrying their age-mark in the right place for the ensuing year. At a glance one could tell a sheep's age by her paint mark; her sire and if she was a twin or single by her ear-nip. Nowadays the experts require an earful of tags and a book full of figures to get the same information – and you have to catch the ewe to get it!

One of the regular members of the shearing gang was always Bobby Burt, one of three brothers who worked on the farm. Their grandfather had moved to Newburgh with Mr William's grandfather in 1870. Bobby, who used to stutter somewhat, was a great character and a firm favourite with the governor. One year we were shearing ewe lambs on Derby Day. Billy Boss was in the office across the yard and Bobby, who had put money on a horse, brought his wireless back after dinner to listen to the race.

About five minutes before the start, he switched off the motor and we all sat down on the wool sacks with a cup of tea to listen to the race. Just as the horses came under starter's orders, Billy Boss, having heard the engines stop, came bustling into the barn. He stopped short on seeing everyone sitting down. "Whatever has gone wrong?" he enquired. "N-n-nothing," replied Bobby, "B-b-but there b-b-bloody well will be if you d-don't b-b-bide quiet." Wherever he was there was sure to be some nonsense going on.

A large flock of laying hens was kept on free range under the care of the head gardener, Jim Baggs, and members of the staff were able to purchase the cracked misshapen eggs very cheaply. One day, I went to pick up a tray of these eggs and Bobby followed me into the old dairy where they were washed, packed and stored. "I w-wants a t-t-tray of c-c-cracked ones, Jim," he called, only to receive the answer: "I ain't got no more." Bobby winked at me, took his pocket knife from his trouser pocket and, holding it by the blade, proceeded to tap a whole tray of eggs, cracking every one. Returning his knife to his pocket, he poked his head around the door into the next room where Jim was busy washing eggs at the sink. "Y-y-you has a t-t-trayful now. I-I-I'll have they."

Bobby used to drive one of the combines at harvest and this was about the only time of year that Billy Boss went on the rampage. He used to have the off-side door taken off his Land Rover so that it was easier and quicker to get in and out. He then used to commute between the combines and the dryer at high speed. A breakdown of either would bring him tearing down like the wrath of the gods.

Using relief drivers, the combines were kept going at mealtimes but the governor would never go to his own lunch until the regular drivers had taken over again. On one occasion they were cutting a piece of barley about half a mile straight up the farm road and in full view of the yard. For some reason Bobby had been taking a lot of stick from Billy Boss all morning and was somewhat peevish. As soon as he took over the combine again the governor departed for his own lunch in a cloud of dust, leaving Bobby to carry on. "Y-y-you watch me g-g-give him d-d-diarrhoea," grunted Bobby as he drove off. Just as the Land Rover stopped in the distant yard, Bobby stopped the combine, got down and lay beneath it. Alighting from his Land Rover, Billy Boss glanced back to check if all was well, only to see the outfit had stopped. Out came his field-glasses, to reveal Bobby tinkering about underneath it. The long-suffering Land Rover did a vicious U-turn and came back up the hill like a bat out of hell but, as it turned into the field, the combine moved off again. The governor jumped onto the machine as it passed him and, climbing up to Bobby, enquired what the trouble had been. "N-n-nothing much," came the reply. "S-s-she's j-j-just a bit awk'ard like some p-p-people I k-k-know."

Bobby was always a beater on shooting days. On one occasion, as they were preparing for the first drive, Billy Boss was placing the walking guns with a beater between each gun. "You like to go next to Mr Tory?" he enquired of Bobby. "N-n-not b-b-bloody likely! That l-l-long legged b-b-bugger shoots too s-s-straight." Bobby did not relish the idea of having to carry too many hares. Mr Jim Tory was, and still is, a very good shot.

Tom Dove, one of the tractor drivers, used to catch moles in his spare time, being paid so much per tail for doing so. A field on the north side of the main road, consisting of very peaty soil, had been re-seeded and the moles were heaving it up and making a real mess. Bobby was sent to roll it down so that Tom could see where to put his traps. The moles were heaving when he got there and before he started rolling he managed to kick out nine or ten, cut their tails off, then let them go again. Tom put down his traps the next day only to catch moles without tails. No tails – no money!

There was another side to Bobby. A first class tractor driver, there was no job on the farm he could not do. If required, he would help in the dairy or with the sheep. If the cattle got out or there was a bad calving Bobby was always available, regardless of the time. I remember having a ewe with a complete prolapse of the uterus after lambing on a cold, wet December night. The ewe must have weighed at least two hundredweight and I had to have help to hold her up while I got the womb back into place and stitched her up. A call under Bobby's window was all that was needed; in a few minutes he was down and we got on with the job.

Our show season started with the Devon County in mid-May, but preparations had started a long time before that. People often ask me how soon I start preparing a sheep for show. My answer is always the same – about five months before it is born. First of all, the animal has to be bred right, then it has to be fed properly and, lastly, trimmed and brought out as near to perfect as is humanly possible. We used to pick out about twenty of our best lambs with their mothers when the lambs were about a month old and these were kept in a separate fold and pushed on as hard as we dared go. We often swapped them round, bringing in a few fresh ones that caught our eye and turning out the odd one or two that had not grown on as well as we would have wished. The shearling rams and ewes that we intended to show were brought inside just after Christmas, shorn out in early January and kept housed until April. Although we did not actually start to prepare the show sheep until early May, a tremendous amount of extra work had already been put into them. Two to three weeks before the show both the lambs and shearlings were backed out and their back ends shaped. They were then washed, left for a week and trimmed three or four times in the week prior to the show. Bobby Mitchell used to reckon that a sheep was fit to put into the ring when, after it was trimmed all over, the wool cut off would go into a match box. I still endeavour to maintain that standard today.

The trimming really divided itself into two parts. First comes the actual cutting of the wool into the shape you want (which is almost like sculpting). The sheep's back is cut out flat and straight to give it a good top line and the flattened back enhances its width. The backside is cut out to create the illusion of meat bulging over its hocks. The chest is also flattened to make the animal's front end look wider. The second part of the trimming consists of what I call "facing". The fleece consists of thousands of little curls of wool, each curl made up of hundreds of individual fibres. These are all of slightly different lengths. First of all, you comb out the fleece with a special carding comb, consisting of hundreds of wire staples set in a leather back. They protrude about half an inch through the leather, being slightly bent and pointed. When drawn through the fleece these combs break up the curls and pull the fibres out to their maximum length. The tips are then trimmed off with the shears and, after doing this several times, all the fibres have been teased out and cut off to exactly the same length which gives a solid, almost felt-like appearance to the fleece.

Trimming is something of an acquired art and it takes a great deal of practice before one becomes proficient. It is also one of the things in life that I never tire of doing and I still get a great thrill from turning out a good sheep well. The bulk of trimming was always done at home, leaving just a final touch-up on judging morning. We always travelled to shows the day before judging, with the exception of the Royal and Smithfield, where we allowed ourselves an extra day to get the sheep settled in. After the final trim at home, the sheep were sheeted up in canvas coats to keep them clean whilst travelling and also to hold their fleeces together. All this had to be done by lunch-time on the day prior to travelling as we always had an inspection by Mrs Hooper (Mr Tom's widow) in the afternoon. She would arrive with her daughter, Joy, at about half past two, coming straight around to the trimming shed behind the shearing barn. After a courteous greeting to Arthur and me she always asked the same question. "Got anything useful?" On being assured that we had, she asked to see them. By this time, Billy Boss would have joined the party.

First out was always the best single ram lamb. I would stand him in the centre of the yard as though in a judging ring. The good lady then proceeded to go over him with a fine tooth comb. If he had a fault it was spotted in a moment. Then, with Arthur, she would compare him with lambs of the past – when those two got together it was really the deep calling the deep. The same procedure was followed with the second single ram lamb. Then the pen of three were brought out, with Mr William, Joy and me holding them. This was a class that, over the years, the Newburgh flock had a great reputation for winning and we used to be able to match them like peas in a pod. After going over them with Arthur, Mrs Hooper would ask for the spare lamb to be brought out, to see if it matched any better. I remember on one occasion the spare lamb was down a little on both back pastern joints, this being the reason why he had not been included in the show team.

Before I had time to line it up with the other three, I was told to put it back. I politely enquired why, at which Mrs Hooper snorted: "If the poor devil had three straight legs it would not be so bad, but he has only got two." She never missed a trick.

The highlight of the afternoon came – the pen of three ewe lambs. They were handled, walked around, argued over, swapped about to see which one had to stand in the middle and then finally approved. After thanking both of us she would go in to tea with Mr William.

The Monday following the show, without fail, Joy would drive up to the sheep fold with an envelope for each of us. Enclosed were two notes, one thanking and congratulating us, the other green (one pound), but if the ewe lamb had won (as quite often happened), it was blue (five pounds). According to Arthur, the ewe lambs had always been Mrs Hooper's favourites. We used to show shearling rams and ewes as well but she had no interest in them whatever and never asked to see them.

Our show team usually consisted of eight lambs and four shearlings: two single ram lambs, a pen of three and a pen of three ewe lambs, two single shearling rams and two single shearling ewes. As we were away from home for four or five days at most shows, a considerable amount of food and tackle had to be taken. The sheep food consisted of corn, mangolds, vetches and hay. There was a show trough which could be hung on the hurdles for each pen, plus buckets, trimming tackle and a small root cutter for the mangolds. We also had to take the Calor gas cylinder, cooker, camp beds and sleeping bags and last, but most important, the show box in which were packed our personal effects, food and a supply of medicines for the sheep in case anything went wrong. The deck boards in the lorry were let down and a rick sheet spread over them to stop any dust falling down onto the sheep. The food and tackle were packed on it and the bottom of the lorry was bedded up a foot deep with clean straw. Then we were ready to load – the rams at the front and the ewes behind – and away we went, hoping nothing had been forgotten.

The first show was always the worst to get ready for as all the sheep had to be trimmed from the rough and the tackle hunted out and cleaned up. By this time, most of the major shows had moved onto permanent sites which meant that the facilities for both animals and attendants had improved.

Judging usually started at nine-thirty. Billy Boss and Arthur would arrive just before nine. If the weather was at all chilly the governor would be wearing a dark suit and bowler hat, but if it looked like being a hot day he was always attired in flannels, linen coat and straw hat.

Arthur would greet his old mates and have a quick look round the opposition. His most optimistic prediction would be: "Might get a card 'reckly with a bit of luck." At that time the Dorset Downs were very popular and in great demand as crossing sires. There would be upwards of a dozen flocks competing at all the major shows. The first time I went to the Bath and West, there were thirty-four single ram lambs and fourteen pens of three. Bringing them out were what I would describe as the last generation of great Dorset Down shepherds: Frank Radford, Dennis Buckingham, Fred Sturney, Tom Amey, Jimmy Lovell, Shep Samson, Fred Dunford, Dick Knight and Bobby Mitchell. To spend an evening in their company, listening to them expounding the art and mystery of the shepherd's calling, was an education which would be impossible to obtain today. They were very jealous of their knowledge and, if asked, would rarely reveal any of their secrets, but if you kept your ears and eyes open and your mouth shut, you learned a lot, especially as their mood expanded in direct proportion to their consumption of brown ale.

Judging over, the owner of the Champion took the flock masters and shepherds to the bar for a celebration drink. This usually ended in quite a session. During the remainder of the show, most of the time was spent around the pens, which was when and where the business was done. We sold the odd sheep or two but mostly we chatted up any potential buyers and met many of our established customers. They were invited to go into the pens and handle the sheep. This was really an exercise in public relations and we did our best to impress them with what we had for sale.

One year, for some reason, Billy Boss was greatly taken with a big, long, dark ugly ram and in spite of (or perhaps because of) our disapproval, bought it. We got it home but did not put it out to work. After about a fortnight, he read the riot act and insisted that it be used. It was running with a few spare stud rams that were clearing up the last of the vetches under Coombe Wood. I used to look round the sheep last thing at night but on this occasion, Arthur volunteered to see the stud rams and, in spite of my assurance that it was no trouble, he insisted on doing it himself.

As he deposited his dinner bag in the sheep house the next morning, he announced quite casually, "Shan't have to put thick ram out after all."

"Why?" I enquired.

"'Cause the bugger dead on his back," he replied with obvious relish. After a moment the penny dropped.

"When you went back last night you tipped the damn thing up."

"What if I did?" came the reply. "I ain't going to have a kite like that used on my ewes."

Billy Boss came around just before breakfast and asked the usual question: "Everything all right?"

"No," said Arthur. "Got some bad news for thee. Thick thing that thee bought at Fair were dead on his back this morning. He were all right when I looked over hurdles last thing yesterday." The governor moaned a bit and departed homeward.

"I thought you told Billy Boss he were all right when you went there last night?" I enquired.

"So he were," came the answer, "but I didn't tell him what he were like when I left!"

By the end of June, the vetches were finished, the ewes lambed and the ewes moved on into grass aftermath, generally after a cut of silage had been taken in May. The rams went into either peas or spring vetches for about a month and then, by the first week in August, they were into a piece of early sown kale, which used to last them until they were all sold by mid-October.

The sales over, we used to have a month to six weeks of comparative ease. With all the rams sold, this left the three hundred ewes and about one hundred and fifty ewe lambs. These two flocks were folded on grass, which greatly reduced the workload. After carrying hurdles through knee-high kale, vetches and peas for five months, it was child's play to swing three hurdles on your back and carry them forward through soft grass six inches high, with nothing to catch either your feet or the hurdles and trip you up. It was so much easier to punch a hole with the fold bar in the dense turf than in loose arable, which kept running back into the hole as fast as it was made. This was a time of relaxation and preparation for the next season. We used to cut and sharpen several hundred hurdles and wire shores which were growing in Coombe Wood. They were mainly hazel and ash saplings about two or three inches in diameter, five feet long and pointed at the bottom end. The wire shores had a cut nail driven in a foot from the point and left protruding an inch, which held the bottom of the wire down: a second nail six inches from the top of the shore held the top up.

The hay cribs were out by early November and the ewes were given a feed first thing in the morning before being let forward into their fresh fold. We used the old-fashioned split ash cribs: two dozen for the ewes and a further dozen for the ewe lambs – our "hoggs" as we called them by now. Like the hurdles, the cribs were moved forward each day. I used to carry the bales of hay into the fold, put them down by the cribs and cut the strings. While I did this Arthur would fill the cribs with hay using a short-stemmed, two-pronged pick. As soon as I started to carry in the hay the dogs would jump the hurdles and drive the sheep back to the top end of the fold, keeping them there until we had finished filling the cribs. When this was done, the dogs were called out and the sheep went back to their hay. The same procedure was carried out when we started feeding corn to the in-lamb ewes. We filled the troughs while the dogs held them back and woe betide any old ewe that tried to get past them. To try and fill troughs with three hundred-odd ewes milling around would have been impossible.

The lambing pen was always erected during November. Arthur insisted that it be ready a fortnight before lambing was due to start, in case anything went wrong. Then came one more show before it started all over again – Smithfield, held at Earls Court in London.

It never ceases to amaze me how people behave in London. Everyone seems to be in such a hurry. When I travel on the underground they are running and rushing about to catch the trains. I can understand anyone running to catch the bus in the village because if you miss it, you have to wait until next week for another. But on the underground there is a train every few minutes, and yet people rush around as if their lives depended on it. The one thing that my annual stay in London brings home to me is how lucky I have been all my life to be able to live, bring up a family and earn my living in the countryside.

To look out over London from the top floor of Earls Court on a cold, wet, December morning at the endless miles of roof-tops with not a patch of grass in sight makes me realise why city people attach so much importance to getting away to the countryside for a holiday – and why so many move down to our part of the country on retirement. Undoubtedly there is a lot more money to be earned in the metropolis, but give me Dorset any day.

The great thing about going to Smithfield for a week is returning home. When I go outside the next morning, instead of the constant roar of the traffic, the smell of petrol and diesel fumes and the unyielding concrete or tarmac to walk on, there are the sounds of the countryside: the "caw-caw" of the rooks flying overhead on their way to raid a late-sown piece of wheat, the deep mutter of the ewes and the shrill call of an early born lamb or two. These things, together with the fresh, sweet smell of hay as you fill the hay cribs and the feel of the soft, damp earth under your feet, suddenly make you realise that there is a lot more to life than money.

I have tried to describe the yearly round of the hurdled shepherd as I remember it in the 1960s. It was an agricultural practice that tied in with the old four-course arable rotation which had been the established method of farming over the downland of southern England for over a hundred years, a practice that has now sadly ceased to exist, being superseded by the use of artificial fertilisers and chemical sprays. It is my considered opinion that no way has yet been found to produce sheep as healthy and of a quality and hardiness to compare with the old hurdled system.

Parasites are one of the great scourges of the modern sheep farmer. Many shepherds drench their flocks for worms every three weeks during the summer months with the modern, effective and expensive worm drenches.

Arthur spent over fifty years with the Newburgh flock and in all that time the sheep were never drenched for worms and never needed to be. They were in the same field only one year in four and then had a fresh patch each day. Sheep were born in temporary straw-thatched lambing pens and spent their entire life out of doors, never being housed at all. This in itself produced animals with a great hereditary hardiness. In the winter of 1963 the snow came down on Christmas night with drifts six and eight feet deep. We were almost finished with the lambing and had well over three hundred lambs all aged under one month, with many only a week or two old, most of which had been turned out of the lambing pens. They stayed out during that long, bitterly cold winter, when the snow still remained under the hedges in March, yet our losses could be counted on the fingers of two hands.

After the initial fall of snow on that Christmas night, we were two ewes and two lambs short. All our efforts to find them failed and the only place we reckoned they could be was under the hedge that ran behind the lambing pens, where the drifts were six feet deep on the Sunday afternoon. Nine days later, Billy Boss came along at around three o'clock in the afternoon as we were feeding up and went down under the hedge yet again, spiking into the snow with a long cane to see if he could find them. We heard him shouting and when we went to see what was wrong he had disappeared into the drift. The two ewes and their lambs were alongside the hedge: the snow had swept over them and formed an igloo some six feet square and just enough for them to stand up in. The bank had been completely stripped of vegetation and they had eaten the bark off the sticks in the hedge. By walking over the top of the sheep, Billy Boss had caused the snow roof to collapse and he had fallen down beside them. The snow was so deep he could not look out over the top. We dug away the side of the drift, making a ramp on which we laid a couple of hurdles. The two ewes walked up and Billy Boss scrambled out behind them with a lamb under each arm. They all survived and after a few days seemed none the worse for their ordeal. Nowadays, when I see ram breeders keeping their ewes and lambs inside from December to March, I often think of those little lambs and their mothers who were buried in the snow for nine days and who walked away from it fit and healthy.

It would not be right to conclude this account of the Newburgh flock without trying to sum up the two men, Billy Boss and Arthur: one who had helped to make the flock what it was and the other who had kept it so. Perhaps I have not drawn them quite fairly and if this is the case, I apologise. They each had their funny little ways and I seem to have written chiefly about these but they were both, in their own way, masters of their profession.

I owe a great deal to these two gentlemen, especially Arthur, who instilled in me so much of the art of shepherding. I thought that I knew my job inside out before I went to Newburgh, but from Arthur I learned the truth of the saying: "You are never too old to learn if you are not too stubborn to be taught." I am pleased to say I was not the latter; but like a young dog working with an old one, I also picked up some of his less desirable tricks. I'm afraid I have never treated any of my bosses with the same regard or respect since coming under his influence!

We were folding a piece of clover with the ram and ewe lambs in May one year; the boss wanted to pull them out and go into the vetches so that he could cut the remaining clover for silage. Arthur decided that the vetches were not fit and refused to move. "I knows they b'ain't fit, thee knows they b'ain't fit; if thee uncle were alive he would not go into 'em for another fortnight. But then he were a proper farmer!" Faced with this argument the governor withdrew, but after breakfast he sent the foreman up with orders that we had to move out. Now this was asking for trouble, as the foremen had no authority over the shepherds. The foreman was quite aware of this and rather shamefacedly gave his message that we were to move out on Friday morning. Arthur was a big man, just over six feet tall and about fifteen stone. He drew himself up to his full height. "Now, thee go back and tell Bill Boss, with my compliments, mind, that if he ain't got the guts to pull the trigger he got no bloody business loading the gun." The lambs stayed in the clover for another fortnight.

On another occasion a load of hay had been brought up to the sheep. It was badly rain-washed and mouldy and the ewes refused to eat it. When Bill Boss came up the next morning Arthur took him over to the hay pen. "My ewes b'ain't eating this tack," he growled. "Mouldy as a cat's turd – starve a blasted billy goat."

The governor took a look. "Well, you will have to get rid of it now it's up here. I'll send up some better when it has gone." He turned and walked towards the gate.

Arthur pulled a box of matches from his pocket and lit the hay. "That won't be no trouble," he grinned.

Bill Boss ran back and beat out the fire, but after breakfast a load of good hay appeared and the rough was hauled away. I suppose that all this may sound rather childish but, as far as Arthur was concerned, they were *his* sheep and he was immensely proud of them. He would do anything he thought necessary for their well-being, even to the point of upsetting the governor; and he took as a personal affront any criticism which he considered to be unjustified.

For several years, Dr Parry visited the flock every six months in connection with research that he was carrying out into scrapie. One year he paid us a visit a few days before lambing started, arriving just before lunch. The ewes had filled themselves out and, being heavily in lamb, looked a picture. Dr Parry made the initial mistake of not greeting Arthur in the manner to which he was accustomed. "Anyone would think we was somat the dog dragged in," Arthur muttered, as we followed Billy Boss and the doctor into the fold.

The good doctor walked around the ewes for a few minutes and then he started: "Mr William, these sheep are far too fat," he exclaimed, and kept enlarging on it as he walked through the flock. By this time Arthur had started to scuffle his boot in the grass and change his crook from hand to hand – sure signs that an explosion was not far off. Billy Boss read the danger signals and diplomatically began to steer the doctor towards the Land Rover. At the hurdles, as he went out, Dr Parry turned and addressed Arthur and me in what I assumed was the same manner in which he spoke to his students. Unfortunately Arthur was no student. "There is no need whatever to get in-lamb ewes looking like this," the doctor snapped. "They are far too fat, and I would hate to have to lamb them."

"Too fat, be damned," roared Arthur. "As for lambing 'em, thee wouldn't be man enough for the job any road. Teaching students to be as daft as theeself be 'bout your mark." That was the last time we ever saw the doctor. This little story is so typical of Arthur: criticise his ewes and God help you.

Like Arthur, Billy Boss had his funny little ways. He also had his big, generous ones. On being congratulated after a good win or sale, he always made it abundantly clear that it was the shepherd, not himself, who should take the credit. Whenever he won a championship, as soon as the cards and rosettes had been given out, he would walk across the ring, raise his hat to the judge and, shaking hands with Arthur and me, would congratulate us in front of everyone. His big ways were magnificent.

The Romneys

THERE are times in life when you get itchy feet and the grass looks greener on the other side of the fence. This happened to me in 1969 and we moved to Rye, in East Sussex, where I became farm manager of a six hundred acre holding on the edge of Romney Marsh. Looking back I must have been off my head to exchange the lovely rolling countryside of West Dorset for the flat, bleak expanse of the Marsh, where the wind never goes round, but straight through you; but it was an experience that I would never have missed. David had just left school and came to work with me before going to Agricultural College. We were allowed to establish our own small flock of Southdowns and we made a lot of new friends.

The farm was typical of the Romney Marsh area, with the exception of about a hundred acres that immediately surrounded Camber Castle. This ruined castle had been built in the reign of Henry VIII, as a coastal defence against the French. When constructed it was right on the edge of the coast, but over the years the bay had silted up and today it stands a good mile inland. The land just around it has only a couple of inches of soil over the top of pebbles. It dried out quickly in summertime, remained fairly dry regardless of the weather and was excellent for wintering sheep. The rest of the farm was heavy loam running to clay. There were no hedges, the fields being divided by large drainage ditches, mostly six to eight feet wide and about the same in depth, with the water levels controlled by a series of hatches. The practice was to raise these during the winter to get the water away as quickly as possible and to lower them in the spring so that the ditches became full. This in turn kept the sheep in and also raised the water table, which kept the grass growing. There was always competition in the early spring with the arable, though: the water needed to be low in the ditches to let the land dry out for corn sowing, but high to keep the sheep in.

About one hundred and twenty acres of corn (half barley, half wheat) and some twenty to thirty acres of roots were grown annually. The rest of the farm was down to grass – one hundred and fifty acres permanent and the rest three-year leys. The main stocking of the farm was one thousand Kent ewes, with two to three hundred ewe tegs and somewhere around eighty to one hundred beef cattle.

It was quite a change from three hundred pedigree Down ewes in hurdles to one thousand commercial ewes on the Marsh.

Here I must say a few words concerning the Romney Marsh sheep, and in so doing hope that I don't offend any of my friends in that part of the world. For many years these sheep have been exported all over the world and their breeders rightly claim that the sun never sets on the Romneys. They have been especially successful in New Zealand, having played a major part in the sheep production of that country.

Romneys could be described as the shortest-woolled of the long-woolled breeds. Having been bred for many generations in the unique conditions of the area, with its cold, harsh, winter climate yet luxuriant summer grazing, coupled with a comparatively low rainfall, the sheep have developed an ability to thrive when densely stocked on permanent pasture and have a great resistance to parasites. A very docile breed, easily shepherded, they have a remarkable capacity to recover condition in a very short time. They can be lambed down in April as poor as crows and by June, when shorn, they are as fat as pigs. Romneys can be, and in many cases are, farmed with very little labour, hence their popularity all over the world.

Now to the other side of the coin. I firmly believe that every shepherd should lamb a flock of Romneys at least once in his career, then he would realise what lambing is all about. Mind you, they lamb all right, being no more trouble when giving birth than any other breed. It is after they have had their lambs that the fun starts. From the moment she has dropped her lambs, filling her belly has first claim on a ewe's time and looking after her lambs will be well down on her list of priorities. I found that the majority had enough milk to rear a single well but not enough to make a good job of twins. In any case, they had no intention of rearing two if it was possible to lose one somewhere down the line. A ewe with twins a couple of days old could be turned onto a bite of grass; down would go her head and away she went. Most breeds of ewe with young lambs keep grazing comparatively near where their young are lying down. Not so the old Romney – she walks two steps between each bite. If she is put at one end of a ten-acre field she will be at the other end in half an hour, leaving her lambs to look after themselves. When they get hungry and let out their piteous little "baas", instead of returning to them, calling all the way, as any civilised ewe would do, she will lift her head between mouthfuls, let out a deep mutter and resume eating. If the lambs do not go to mother, mother is too idle to go and look for them. In other words, they are shocking mothers.

The first year I lambed them I walked miles and spent hours walking around the couples, picking up one of a twin which had lost its mother, finding her, coupling them up and watching it suck, only to find the next morning

111

that she had lost the other one. There she would be, stuffing her belly, not caring a damn that she had only one lamb instead of two. After about a week, when the lambs had become strong enough to run around and find their mothers, they were all right – but there were times when I could have quite cheerfully shot those Romney ewes. Perhaps I have been a trifle unfair. After lambing Down ewes for years I may have become spoilt, but I still remember picking up and sorting out all those little lambs that the ewes were too idle to mother properly.

After Christmas, the ewes were put onto the dry land around the castle and as soon as the grass became short they were fed hay and concentrates. The ram was put out on Bonfire Night, so lambing started on April 1st. This took place in the open, as only ewes and lambs who were on the weak side were brought inside. The dry land, which was situated in the middle of the farm, consisted of two large fields, each of over forty acres. Once lambing got under way all the ewes were put into one of these fields, where they were fed concentrates first thing in the morning, and they had hay available in the racks all the time. During the early afternoon all the ewes which had not lambed were drifted on into the other field, leaving behind all those who had lambed during the past twenty-four hours. The next day, after breakfast – by which time the lambs were strong enough to run on with their mothers – they were quietly driven into an adjoining field, where a pen had been erected just inside the gate, into which the ewes and lambs were driven. Then the lambs were caught, tailed and castrated before being led out. This left the lambing field empty, ready for the in-lamb ewes to be turned back into it after dinner. Someone was constantly walking round the ewes from first light until dark, giving assistance to any sheep that were in trouble and bringing in any that needed shelter.

After the thatched hurdle lambing and nursery pens of the Downs, this outside lambing seemed very rough and ready, but it was the way it had been done for years. It seemed to work out quite well if the weather was reasonable, but if wet and cold (and we generally managed to get a few days like that, even in mid-April), it was, to say the least, very miserable for both man and beast. If one tells the truth it could be bloody awful. Imagine kneeling down with your coat off assisting a ewe in a windswept field with the rain bucketing down. I made a resolution when I left Kent that never again would I attempt to lamb a flock outside and I never have. The busiest day we ever had was when one hundred and three ewes lambed in twenty-four hours and, as perhaps you have guessed, that day it was raining.

Camber Castle was open to the public and was quite a tourist attraction, especially during the summer and on bank holidays, when a steady trickle of people would be walking through the yard and along the footpath to the castle. One Easter Monday, in the middle of lambing, as I came into dinner I noticed a ewe had just started to lamb alongside the footpath just outside the yard gate. Within a few minutes a very irate middle-aged lady came knocking at the door, demanding that I go out and see to this ewe. I assured her that I had just seen the animal and all was well, but she was most insistent and informed me that the sheep was obviously in great pain and making the most terrible noise, to which I replied: "Madam, if you were doing the same job as that sheep you would be making just as much noise and a damn sight more fuss." Then the penny dropped and, without another word, she fled.

Shearing started the first week in June and here I must give credit where credit is due. I have shorn most breeds of sheep during my life but I reckon that there is nothing to compare with a Romney when it comes to shearing.

When the grease is up you can fairly make them fly, and with their well-sprung ribs, clean faces and legs they are a shearer's dream. The wool was handled in a very different way from that of the Down sheep, for the fleeces were about double the weight and the staple was much longer. The Down fleeces were rolled and tied with a special wool cord and then packed into wool sheets. These sheets were very large sacks, open along one side, and would hold some forty fleeces. When full they were sewn up with a bag needle and string and taken by haulier to the wool staplers for grading. The Romney fleeces were also rolled, but in the following manner: a fleece would be spread out on the floor with the outside uppermost, both sides were turned in until it was about eighteen inches wide and then it was rolled up, starting at the tail end and working up to the shoulder. Then, instead of tying with string, a strip of neck wool was pulled out and twisted round and round until it formed a band which was wrapped tightly around the fleece. The end was tucked back under, giving it the appearance of a Swiss roll tied around the middle. These fleeces were stacked in a large heap at one end of the barn until shearing was completed. When instructed by the wool staplers, they were loaded in a cattle lorry and taken to Ashford for grading.

On arrival, the lorry was backed into the grading shed and the tailgate dropped onto a stool so that it served as a platform. A long table was placed at the back of the lorry, on the end of the tailgate, and half a dozen very large wicker baskets (much like over-sized laundry baskets) were put on either side of the table. The fleeces were tossed from the lorry to the tailgate, to be caught and tossed onto the table. A wool grader stood on either side of the table and as a fleece dropped in front of them they would, by feel and sight, grade it and drop it into the appropriate basket, each basket holding a different grade of wool. As soon as a basket was filled it was taken away and replaced by another, the wool then being baled up to await sale by auction.

The accuracy with which the graders worked was amazing. As far as possible the ewe fleeces were kept separate from the tegs and rams, but if one got mixed up the grader would know in an instant. By mere feel they could tell if a fleece came off a ewe, teg or ram. It was quite uncanny, as was the speed at which they worked – as fast as they were tossed down they were graded.

A public footpath ran from the building at one end of the farm, by the house, across to the castle and then on down from one end of Rye to the other, passing through six fields and for almost half its length running alongside the River Brede. At weekends in the summer most of the cattle and sheep had to be moved off these fields as the gates were always being left open and the sheep and cattle getting mixed up. There was no excuse for this as all the gates were properly hung and could be opened, closed and fastened with ease. Many people seem to think that these rights of way are a birthright; if so, it is a great pity that they don't respect them as such and not regard them as something which is there for their personal convenience. They may only appear to be green fields, but it should always be remembered that they are also someone's livelihood.

The bottom field, nearest the town, was long and narrow, being less than a hundred yards wide for its entire length, with the river on one side and the castle ditch on the other. One Saturday evening at about eight o'clock the phone rang; it was a neighbour to say that about a dozen motor-cyclists were setting up camp in the bottom of this field. David and I drove down to find several tents pitched up and everyone making themselves at home. I asked what the devil they thought they were doing, and reminded them that they were on private property without permission. They replied to the effect that they were doing no harm and had no intention of moving. Realising that persuasion was not going to work, and with odds of ten to one against us, we drove off.

David enquired if they were going to be allowed to stay. "Don't be so damned silly", I snapped. "We be going to get some reinforcements." He looked puzzled but decided that I was not in the best of moods so remained silent. In the next field up we had some twenty-odd eighteen-month to two-year-old steers – and we had old Bob with us now, the biggest, strongest collie that we have ever had and a grand, steady dog with sheep. He had never worked cattle before we came to Kent and had got himself kicked rather badly the first time he was used on them, something he never forgot and never forgave.

We opened the gate and put the old boy away, and he raced around those cattle like a bat out of hell, snapping at their hocks as he went. With Bob in hot pursuit, the steers shot through the gate and down across the field; it was like a cattle stampede in a Wild West movie. We drove along quietly in the rear. The bikers spotted the cattle when they were about two hundred yards from their camp. There were yells of "Bulls, bulls" and shrieks from the girls, several of whom had retired into the tents. It was quite fascinating, by the way, to see what they wore under their leathers – in most cases it seemd to be very little! They all bolted for the gate, leaving the tents unattended. At the last moment, and for once getting it right, I sent Bob forward and headed the cattle just before they got to the camp.

I wandered across and apologised for the cattle getting out, suggesting that some damn fool holidaymaker must have left the gate open and that they were very lucky that we had been there and had been able to stop them before they did any damage. I also suggested that perhaps it would be safer if they moved on in case it happened again. We drove the cattle quietly back the way they had come and within twenty minutes tents, bikes and bikers had disappeared.

The face of Romney Marsh has changed a lot during the last twenty years. It started when we were living there, for the arable was already beginning to make increasing inroads on the permanent pasture. Even so, it was possible to drive from Rye through Brookland, Benzett, Ivychurch and Newchurch on to Hythe in the summer and almost every field would be white with sheep. The density at which they were stocked had to be seen to be believed. One of our neighbours, who became a great friend and helped me quite a lot, was the late Jack Merricks. His yardstick on stocking sheep in the summer was to toss a shilling as far as he could, then if he could walk straight to it and pick it up, the stocking rate was right; if he had to hunt for it in the grass he would either put more sheep in or gang-mow the field. This may sound a rather drastic way to go about things but he was for many years one of the most successful livestock and arable farmers on the Marsh.

The increase in the arable was a direct result of drainage conditions. The ditches were lowered, pumps were installed and miles of tile drains laid. This lowered the water-table and the land would then grow very heavy crops of grain and potatoes, which gave a far greater financial return than could be obtained from sheep. Most lowland areas in England have seen dramatic increases in arable in the last two decades and Romney Marsh has been no exception.

Although many of the flock masters had a great many pure Romney ewes, they only had a percentage of them registered. It was also possible to have pure-bred ewes accepted for registration after being approved by an

117

inspection panel. The flock at Camber Castle had never been registered, although only registered rams had been used for a number of years. During my first summer we had some of our best ewes inspected and approved for registration. The following year we took lambs to Birmingham Fat Stock Show and Smithfield, winning on both occasions. We came back from Smithfield on a Friday evening and prepared another team for Ashford on the following Monday.

My governor had never showed before and winning at Smithfield first time out put the cat among the pigeons; a few of the old hands were not too happy. Out we went on Monday morning. There were two classes for Romneys – one for a pair of wether lambs and the other for a pair of ewe lambs. We won both. This really stirred things up and for the only time in my life I had an objection raised against me. Our sheep had been washed and trimmed out properly, but none of the others had been touched. The head sheep steward informed me that an objection had been raised because my sheep were the only ones to have been washed and trimmed and it was considered unfair competition. I replied to the effect that the other entrants had the same opportunity to wash and trim as I did and that there was nothing in the prize schedule to prohibit either. Off he went, returning with a schedule, and after diligently reading it from one end to the other, admitted that I was right and the awards would stand. We went out for the Inter-breed Championship, which David won with the Southdowns, and I had Reserve with the Romney wethers.

Later, when we were having the traditional drink in the bar, the subject came up again and the Society President started to belly-ache about trimming Romneys. I had had a few to drink by then and had reached the stage when I did not care what I said or to whom I said it. So I reminded him of what another President once said: "If you can't stand the heat then get out of the kitchen," and that it was no good him trying to catch out a man from Dorset, because he did not get up early enough in the morning to do so. He got a bit stroppy at this and told me that things would be different if I came out at the summer shows. Nevertheless, the next year I won with shorn shearling ewes at the Royal.

Through the Kent Branch of the British Herdsmen's Club I got to know several of the Sussex cattle herdsmen quite well, especially Eric Stanley and Royal Norton. Royal was quite a card and always up to some damn fool nonsense. He was also one of the cleverest cattle men I have ever met. He came over to tea one Sunday in late July and in the evening we had a drive round the farm. In a bunch of forward store cattle he spotted a smart, black Sussex cross Friesian steer. He walked around, examining him from all angles, and when he had seen all he wanted he turned to me: "They give a special prize at Ashford Christmas Fat Stock Show for the best beast sired by a Sussex bull. That there steer could win if you pulled your finger out." I replied that with four or five pens of sheep to show I would not have the time and, in any case, I did not know how to do the job properly. "I know that," he chuckled, "but you do just what I tells ee and I'll turn him out and show him."

So, on his instructions, the steer was brought back near the building with a mate for company and fed a little corn outside until September, when they were both brought into a box at night, fed hay and corn and let out to grass during the day. By October they were in all the time, being fed hay, roots, corn and boiled barley. Then we had to train them to lead on a halter. Imagine a two-year-old steer weighing just over half a ton, that had spent its entire life running loose either in a field or a large covered yard,

119

and never been tied up, let alone haltered – and you had to train it to lead. The red steer that we had brought in as a mate for the black one was reasonably easy to handle and after the initial set-to he behaved quite well and was soon leading, but the black was a devil incarnate. Getting a halter on his head was not easy, even when he was put in the crush. Then he would either go round the yard like a mad thing or else refuse to move at any price. We could heave and tug on the halter, twist his tail, give him a clout, but there he would stand, front legs out straight, head down, with no intention of moving at all. Then, suddenly, off he would go like a bullet from a gun, dragging every-one behind him. There were many times when I felt like giving up, but we persevered and one day he just gave up and within a few more days allowed himself to be led quite happily.

We fed him, following Royal's instructions, and washed him twice just before the show. I arrived at Ashford on the Sunday at about two o'clock with the two steers on the back of the lorry and five pens of sheep, plus the grub at the front. The steers were unloaded first, tied up in their places and Royal took charge, leaving me to deal with the sheep and wash out the lorry. By the time I had done this, fed the sheep and put things straight, it was getting on for four o'clock. Then I went up to see how Royal was getting on and found him working on the red steer, which was tied up right at the bottom end of the shed. I had left the black tied up near the top end and as I walked down did not see it and assumed that Royal had moved him. He looked up from clipping out the head of the red steer: "What do you think of the black now I've dolled him up?" he enquired.

"Don't know; I ain't seen him yet; where have you put him?" I asked.

"Not seen him? You just been and walked right past the

damn thing!" came the reply. "He's still in the same place as you put him when we unloaded."

We walked back up the line and sure enough, there he was. But what a change – his back levelled out until it was dead flat and his tail clipped, with the exception of the white end, which was frizzed out into a spotless white fluffy ball of hair. His head and ears were clipped, hooves washed and his entire coat back brushed until he shone. I had not recognised my own bullock, which I had been feeding twice a day for four months. The next morning Royal's prediction came true: he took him out and won.

I also had a wonderful day with the sheep, winning four first prizes, Champion and Reserve Champion. My employer liked to show but would never come out to see the judging, preferring to turn up later in the day. On this occasion I rang him and told him of our successes with both cattle and sheep and he promised to be up within the hour. I suggested that in view of our success some liquid refreshment would be appreciated by all and he agreed to bring some with him. He arrived just before the auction sale was about to begin, by which time most of the stockmen and shepherds had either been celebrating or commiserating for a couple of hours. "I've brought up a few drinks for the lads," he said. "Give me a hand to get them in from the car."

Out we went to the car park and there in the boot was a case of whisky and several bottles of assorted spirits and minerals. I cautioned discretion: "Don't take that lot in yet," I implored. "If they get their hands on it now there won't be any auction. Let it bide until the sale is over."

So at about six o'clock, when the sale had finished and the animals were fed, we duly fetched it in. Royal's brother, Jack, had a massive show box, some four feet long, three wide and the same deep. We used this as a bar. Royal took charge. He purloined a supply of glasses from the caterers and quite a session ensued. As it was the centenary of the show that year, a Royal personage had graced the occasion and presented the prizes. Our Royal had been introduced to him and had subsequently met him several times during the day. He was now coming back through the lines on his way out and spotted Royal weaving about with a bottle of Scotch in his hand, topping up glasses. He stopped, looked at Royal with a grin on his face and said: "You again?"

Royal stopped dead, swayed a little, eyed him up and down and came out with: "I wish you would bugger off home."

"Why?" came the question.

"Because when you are gone I shall be the only Royal man left in Ashford."

The Royal gentleman left roaring with laughter.

Royal was always good for a laugh and the capers he got up to were many and legendary. One one occasion, at the Kent Show, returning around midnight with a party of herdsmen, they walked past the fire station on their way back to the cattle line. Royal announced that during the war he had been in the Auxiliary Fire Service and could drive a fire engine. They climbed aboard, found that the key had been left in the ignition and within a few minutes the appliance was roaring round the main ring, in and out between the jumps, bell ringing and lights flashing, with a crew of cheering cattle men. They were apprehended by the police, while endeavouring to pump out the water jump!

On another occasion, at the Royal Counties, he was again returning to the lines at midnight and decided that the Michelin man (a great rubber balloon, some eight feet tall) which was attached to a forty-foot pole over the Michelin tyre stand, looked lonely, so he decided to take him down. Fetching a long ladder from another stand where they were on display, he placed it against the pole,

Grandmother Baker as a young woman at Croscombe ca. 1880.

Grandfather Baker (left) dressing stone for Wells Cathedral at Doulton ca. 1910.

Yeomanry camp, Priddy, 1904. Uncle Ern is sitting third from right.

Winning cheeses made by Mother at Frome Cheese Show 1905. Farmer Perry to the left.

*Mother at age 18
with Bob Perry
outside
Church Farm Chantry.*

*Dorothy's uncle, grandfather and grandmother in Watton Farm
yard in Bridport 1913.*

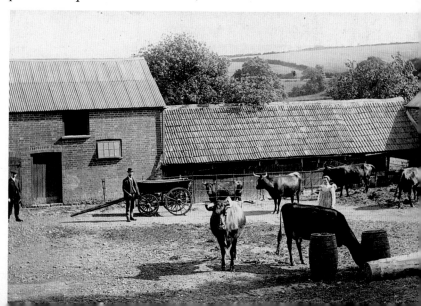

Uncle Bert in Court Farm yard in Litton Cheney ca. 1920.

The author at age five.

Dorothy and her father off to market in the spring wagon. Her brother and mother are to the right.

At Ford Farm in 1941. Dorothy and her brother Jim are to the right. Dorothy's mother (in white) and a niece are on Punch. Another niece stands alongside.

The author with Blossom at the Melplash Show 1955.

Harness room with one season's rosettes. The author with John Wood and his wife 1979.

The author with Captain, winner of the Harness Class at the Vintage Farm Working Event at Beckington 1979.

The author with Fly and Dorset Down ewe lambs passing the school at Halse, Taunton 1959.

Dorset Down shepherds at the Royal Show 1964. Middle row: Frank Radford, third from left; Freddie Dunford, fifth; author at end.

THE NEWBURGH FLOCK IN 1966

Sheep washing. (Above) Billy Boss is pushing the sheep in. Bill King and Bill Vosey are in the background. (Below) Woulty Doulton is in the foreground.

Ewes and lambs in roots (above).   *Ram lambs in clover* (below).

Arthur Whittle in the hay pen with Trimm.

The May Fair entry of Dorset Horn rams from the College of Agriculture 1977.

Judging Jacob sheep at the Royal Cornwall Show 1993. HRH the Princess Royal is looking on.

Shearing with George Payne at Nallers Farm 1975.

Trimming John Briggs's Oxford Down ram at the Royal Show 1981.

*David and Billy Boss with Reserve Champions at the Royal
Show 1967.*

*Father and son with Champion Southdowns and Romneys at
the Ashford Fat Stock Show 1969 . . .*

DOUGLAS LOW

. . . and with First Prize Southdowns and Dorset Downs at the Royal Smithfield Show 1979.

PETER ADAMS

Dorset Down Champion at the Royal Show 1988. Left to right: Breed President Philip Merson, Judge Walter Burroughs, Dorothy and the author.

Dorset Down Breed Champion at the Royal Show 1995. Judge Jim Tory to the left.

Dorothy and the dogs outside Charity Farm House 1995.

The Bride Valley and Litton Cheney.

Sunset at Chilcombe with Bob 1994.

ANDREW SHAYLOR

climbed to the top and was coming down with the balloon when again the long arm of the law caught up with him.

The Sussex herdsmen had a very special drink which they used to brew in the evening after judging. It was known as "Sussex Tea". As a mere shepherd, I was never allowed to discover the intimate details of its preparation – only the outline of how it was brewed.

To be made properly, it had to be prepared in the bucket from which the champion had been fed. This bucket was scrubbed out (or it was supposed to be), partly filled with a gallon to a gallon and a half of water and placed over a primus stove or gas ring until it came to the boil. A quantity of tea, which seemed to be the biggest part of a quarter-pound packet, was tied up in a piece of rag, like a great tea bag, added to the boiling water and stirred until there was half a bucket of very strong, neat tea. The entire operation was in the capable hands of the head brewer, who discharged his duties with dignity and decorum. Milk was added until the tea became the right colour (I never did find out what the right colour was). Then quite a large amount of sugar was poured in and carefully stirred until it had dissolved. At that stage one had a gallon and a half of very strong *sweet* tea!

Then the really serious business of brewing began. The head brewer, watched by the rest of the company, would, with due reverence, add the whisky. This varied from six to eight bottles according to the generosity of the champion's owner. The mixture of tea and whisky was stirred well, the bucket returned to the primus or gas ring, and the heat turned down until the mixture was gently simmering. There was a great art in this simmering; it was reckoned to spoil the lot if allowed to come to the boil. The simmering seemed to go on for about an hour, with the brewer sitting alongside the bucket, stirring gently. After about half an hour he would dip out a little with a mug, blow on it until

123

cool, take a sip, shake his head and return what was left in the mug to the bucket. This tasting continued about every five minutes, until after a little while he would take a second sip and announce: "Getting better." After a few more goes he would proceed to: "Not bad" and finally, after several sips, to: "Just right." Here was none of the finesse of the wine taster – sniffing the aroma, holding a glass to the light and swilling a sip around in the mouth – but a good swig from a mug and the pronouncement that everyone was waiting for: "Just right."

The consuming of the brew had no finesse, either; no delicate glasses, filled from a napkin-held bottle, but mugs dipped into a three-gallon galvanised bucket. But what you received in those mugs was pure nectar, the wine of the gods. The first time I partook of this beverage, when Eric Stanley was in charge, I had watched its preparation with some trepidation. Finally, a half-full mug of the brew was thrust into my hand as we sat around on straw bales. I remember looking at it with some misgiving. It had the appearance of badly over-stewed tea. The Champion was toasted and, shutting my eyes, I took a sip. The result was a pleasant surprise. It tasted quite good. A bigger sip followed, which was even better. I can honestly say that Sussex tea, when properly prepared, is a drink to savour. Mind, it also has a kick like a mule!

Southdowns

THERE are certain things in life that one is proud to have done or been associated with and, for me, Southdown sheep and the Southdown Sheep Society come into this category. I had greatly admired Southdowns for many years. The oldest of our short-woolled breeds, they were improved in the late 1700s by that great Sussex breeder, John Ellman, and subsequently crossed with the local indigenous heath sheep of the south and east of England to produce the Down breeds of today.

These very compact, deep-bodied, short-legged sheep with great hindquarters were, and I contend still are, one of our best producers of quality lamb. Their woolly faces from which their bright eyes peep out, the mouse-coloured nose and tiny ears, give them an aristocratic look. Our elder son, David, had grown up with sheep and from an early age had become very much involved, helping me in the evenings, at weekends and during school holidays. From the age of eleven he'd come to the shows, going to the Bath and West in his Whitsun holidays, having a week off school for the Royal and another for Smithfield. His teacher was not too happy about him taking this time off, but I am sure that in those two weeks a year he learned more about life and the job he had made up his mind he wanted to do – and to which he became dedicated – than he ever would have done at school.

He used to run errands and help several of the older shepherds, who spoiled him shamefully and who, I am sure, helped instill in him the love of sheep and the art of shepherding. When he was twelve we bought him four Southdown wether lambs in September. He fed and looked after them and they were shown at Birmingham Fat Stock Show and later at Smithfield, gaining a third at Birmingham and a highly commended at Smithfield. The enterprise was repeated the next year and, to his great delight, he was in the first three at both shows.

The following year we moved to Rye in East Sussex and with the job came the opportunity to keep a small flock of my own. We decided that they would be Southdowns and that we would avoid buying any sheep that contained imported blood, a resolution that I am proud to say we have kept to this day. An old-established breeder, Mr Charles Goodger, had recently died and his flock was to be dispersed. He had never gone in for showing or ram breeding, but had an extremely good flock of very correct sheep.

It was to his farm at Chidham, just inland from Emsworth on the South Downs, that David and I journeyed on a bitterly cold Saturday morning in January 1968. The flock consisted of one hundred and fifty ewes in regular ages, and we were invited to take our pick. This was a wonderful opportunity and if I did not select the best sheep it was my own fault. I had, on a number of occasions, told other people what I considered was the right way to establish a pedigree flock. Now I had the opportunity to prove myself. I am glad to say that I was prepared to put my money where my mouth was, a decision I have never regretted. We picked out the six teeth ewes, of which there were about forty. From these we selected five of the best, all sired by a Parkgate ram, who was sired by a Ford ram; these five ewes were also in lamb to another Parkgate ram, again by Ford. What we in fact selected were five half-sisters in lamb to the same ram.

126

There was method in my madness. I had always considered that the Ford flock of Walter Langmead had the finest and hardest-fleshed sheep in the breed. This is, of course, only my personal opinion, but our successes over the last twenty-odd years, which include eight Breed Champions at the Royal of England, have convinced me I was right.

These five ewes were the foundation of the Camber Castle flock. Only one female has been purchased since and her purchase is a story on its own. Of the five ewes, one was no good; we lambed her twice and on both occasions she did not give enough milk for her lambs, so she had to go. It's no good trying to flog a dead horse. Three of the others turned out to be extremely good ewes and they and their offspring set us on the right road. The other ewe, Chidham IV, or Granny as she was affectionately called, was the sheep one only ever gets once in a lifetime and not always then. She lived until she was seventeen years old, and during her life she had nine sets of twins and four singles and on eleven occasions her lambs took Champion at either the Royal, South of England, or the Kent Show. The year she was sixteen she had a ram lamb which she reared herself. It went on to the Royal, where it won first prize. She died in her sleep about a fortnight before her lamb was due the next year and we buried her at the bottom of the garden. Virtually all the ewes David has today go back to that grand old lady. It seems unbelievable now, but those five in-lamb ewes cost ten pounds each – that was the price we were asked and that was what we paid – but it was perhaps the best fifty pounds I have ever spent. They settled in and lambed down without any trouble, rearing seven lambs the first year.

The following September we went to Findon Fair, where the Southdown Show and Sale is held, and purchased another Parkgate ram, again by Ford. He was, in fact, a half-brother to the ram by which the ewes were in lamb when purchased. This sheep gave us a great start, in as much as he sired some very good males, but even better females, a thing that is of paramount importance when founding a pedigree flock.

Our first show was the South of England in 1969, where we won first prize for a pair of shearling rams. The late John Craig, one of the great Southdown breeders of his day, congratulated David and asked if, as an older man, he could give him some advice, which was: "Now that you are a pedigree breeder, make haste slowly." I have given the same advice to many aspiring breeders since. Unfortunately, so many want instant success and think they can achieve it if they spend a lot of money. Inevitably they end up a lot poorer and, one hopes, a little wiser. In 1971 we won our first championship at the South of England. I had, during the course of my career, produced a number of champions for my employers and was thrilled and very proud to do so, but to win with your own sheep, that you have bred and reared yourself, is a thing that will stick in my mind forever. We have won many times since, but the first one is never forgotten. In 1975 we had the win that everyone always dreams of – the Royal of England – a shearling ram out of Granny by a ram we had purchased from Roland Harris: Bloxworth D86.

In 1970 we purchased a ram from the Eartham flock. He was a big, strong sheep which gave us quite a bit more size, but his lambs were very heavy in the shoulder and looked over-loaded in front. They had fair back ends, but they looked smaller than they were because of their massive shoulders. At first I was very worried about it and then I remembered what old Frank Radford once told me: "The ass end starts in the shoulder; if you ain't got a shoulder you ain't got no spring of rib; without a spring of

rib you got no loin; without a good loin you got no ass."
How right the old boy was!

Then we had a wonderful stroke of luck, or perhaps it was David's intuition in spotting a maker. With hindsight, and in all honesty, I must admit it was the latter. In May he had gone over to Roland Harris at Bloxworth to buy a shearing machine that was for sale. Now I had always impressed on him that if ever he saw an outstanding ram that he liked he should buy him, regardless of whether we required one at the time or not. David arrived back home with the shearing tackle and announced that he had bought a ram. It transpired that it was a ram lamb only eight weeks old and still on its mother; Roland had agreed to keep it until the first week in September. Thinking that it would have been better to purchase either a shearling or an older stud ram, I proceeded to read the riot act at him for being so silly as to buy a baby lamb still on its mother. He fetched it back one evening in early September and I descended on it with every intention of pulling it to pieces. (You must never let these boys think they know it all!) I tried hard but could find nothing drastically wrong, so I rather grudgingly admitted that I had seen worse. This was Bloxworth D86, who sired three Royal Champions for us and whose sons and grandsons are still doing it to this day. He had great length and back end and when mated with the heavy-fronted ewes by the Eartham ram he produced some really outstanding lambs, especially females. Two of his Champions at the Royal were females, a pair of shearling ewes in 1983 and a pair of ewe lambs the next year. It was these two blood lines, Chidham and Bloxworth, which have been, and still are, the basis of the Camber Castle flock. Bloxworth was the last completely outside-bred ram we ever used. All the rams we have used since have either been of our own breeding or have contained at least fifty per cent Camber Castle blood, for both David and I are ardent believers in line breeding.

Many breeders condemn line breeding, saying that when it is successful it can be called line breeding, but when unsuccessful it becomes inbreeding. I would suggest that when it fails it is because the animals being used are not good enough for the job, in so far as they had some hereditary physical defect, such as under- or over-shot jaws, crooked legs, weak joints, entropion, poor milking ability, bad conformation, etc. If animals with these types of faults are closely bred, trouble is bound to follow, for when two animals with the same genetic weakness are mated, that weakness is certain to be magnified in the offspring. I take the view that, given stock with a sound genetic constitution to begin with, line breeding, or inbreeding, can do no harm.

Many years ago an old Dorset Horn breeder explained how he line bred and why. We still follow his methods to the letter. It does not occur very often, but every now and again a really outstanding ram lamb is born. When this happens (and I must stress he must be *really* outstanding) and providing that both his parents are good sheep, free from any visible faults, we mate him back to his mother; then we watch the offspring from this union grow up for a year, observing it all the time to see if any faults manifest themselves. Here you have to be utterly ruthless. If there is any vestige of doubt that all is not well, you have to stop at once. On the other hand, when things go right the progeny are usually just that bit better than their parents. When this occurred we would keep the ram and work him on any ewes, regardless of how closely they were related, for you cannot get any closer than son to mother; if there were any inherent weaknesses they would be magnified more in that mating than in any other.

I was expounding this theory at an Agricultural Training Board course where there was a well-known Suffolk breeder present. He took the opposite view and advocated the continued use of fresh blood lines. In support of his argument he maintained that the genetics of animals are very similar to those of man, a theory that I entirely agreed with. He then asked if this were the case how could I explain why so many European royal families who had intermarried for generations suffered from insanity. My reply was that it proved my point, for surely the founders of the dynasty had been insane themselves. To achieve power in those days they had to be utterly ruthless, killing, murdering and imprisoning anyone who got in their way; after several hundred years of inbreeding, their insanity had been magnified. On the other hand, in ancient Egypt, the Pharaohs had married their sisters and Cleopatra was the offspring of six generations of such brother/sister marriages. It's the old, old story: "Like breeds like."

I believe that one can learn so much from history and sheep breeding is no exception. Two of the greatest breeders in this country were, without doubt, Robert Bakewell of Dishley Grange, Loughborough (1725–95) and John Ellman of Glynde in Sussex (1753–1832). Bakewell's improved Leicester sheep were used in varying degrees to produce virtually all the long-woolled breeds in England. Likewise, Ellman Southdowns were used to found most of the short-woolled breeds in this country. Both these gentlemen, in founding and greatly improving their respective breeds, line bred extensively. If it was good enough for the two greatest sheep breeders this country has ever known, it has been, and still is, good enough for me.

The first stud ram of our own breeding that we used was in 1975. That year, Granny had twins: one ram, one ewe, both of which were really outstanding. We used the ram lamb, J8, on his mother and then loaned him to Keith Mitchell, who farmed on the Isle of Wight and had recently established a flock of Southdowns, bred by Roland Harris. Subsequently we used J8 successfully for several years on our own ewes and, in the meantime, we acquired one of the rams that he had sired on the Island, Godshill L1. In 1981 this ram sired what I consider to be the finest ram that we ever bred. Not only was he highly successful in the show ring but he has proved to be an outstanding stud ram. He is now nine years old, a little stiff with arthritis, but otherwise hale and hearty and still in regular use. He also has the distinction of being the only ram to which we gave a proper name – "Jasper".

Jasper was shown only once as a ram lamb, winning his class and being placed Reserve Male Champion at the Royal in 1981. The next year as a shearling he was unbeaten, being awarded Breed Champion at the South of England and the Royal. He is a classic example of line breeding. On his sire's side, his great-grandparents were Bloxworth D86 and Chidham 4 (Granny). On his dam's side his grandfather was Bloxworth D86 and his great-grandmother Chidham 4 (Granny).

Jasper T1

Godshill L1		Camber Castle L7	
34961		736496	
Camber Castle	Bloxworth	Bloxworth	Camber Castle
J8	Ewe	D86	A6
Bloxworth	Chidham 4	Parkgate 10	Chidham 4
D86	(Granny)	32111	(Granny)

In advocating line breeding I can only say that the proof of the pudding is in the eating. Despite the fact that our flock has never exceeded twelve ewes, we have, in the last eighteen years, won the Breed Champion at the Royal on eight occasions and in 1986 we could not compete as I was judging. In 1980 and again in 1982 we were awarded both Male, Female and Breed Champions, but what I consider to be the greatest achievement, taking into account the small size of our flock, is that five of our Royal championships have been won with pairs of sheep. This is, to my mind, a clear vindication of the breeding policy. When you can repeatedly bring out matching pairs to beat singles you have got to be right. It is difficult enough to get a single sheep perfect enough to win, but doubly so to get two.

In 1980 David took over the management of the flock and the successes we have had since then are entirely due to him. I know that he will agree with me when I say that neither of us consider we have done anything exceptionally clever or that we have discovered some magic formula to breed or feed sheep. We have, in fact, used the same breeding methods that have been employed successfully for the last two hundred years. We don't use excessive amounts of concentrates. In fact, we use no compound feeds at all, relying entirely on straights; a mixture of oats, peas, beans, flake maize and linseed cake is all we ever use. We still fold, although it is now entirely on grass, but the sheep have a fresh patch every day and the lambs creep on a fold in front of the ewes. The ewes and lambs are only housed for a few days at lambing, spending the rest of the time outside. We don't record weight, use computers or pay some expert to tell us how to do the job, being quite content to carry on in the same way we have always done. I think we make it work as well as some, and better than most.

One of the most gratifying aspects of keeping Southdown sheep has been meeting and becoming friends with so many of the other breeders and shepherds. When we first started I was afraid that we would be the odd ones out, in as much as most of the other flock masters were farmers with, in many cases, large, long-established flocks, whereas I was a professional shepherd with David, who had only just left school, assisting me. In rural areas one is always a little class conscious, and farming is no exception. For a shepherd to start bringing out his own sheep at the major shows was perhaps pushing things a bit, but I had misjudged the Southdown breeders completely. Right from the start they treated us with the utmost courtesy and friendliness, going out of their way to welcome us and put us at ease. For this I would like to say a heart-felt "thank you" and apologise for ever doubting their intentions.

We also had the privilege of meeting and becoming friendly with two of the traditional Southdown shepherds, Jack Coleman of Ringmer and old Shep Oliver, who was at Eartham and whose brother had been at Chidham when we purchased our foundation ewes. They were shepherds of the old school, having spent all their working lives on the South Downs, and for most of the time with Southdown sheep. They both, in their own quiet, dignified, unassuming ways, were a great help to David and me. To spend an hour in their company was to gain a mine of information concerning the breed over the last fifty years. Shep, as tough and weather-beaten as the downs where he had spent his life, was a man of few words. If asked his opinion of a sheep, he would handle it and then pronounce judgement, which was always one of two answers: "Good sheep" or "No good" – no explanation, no half measures, no hesitation – it was one or the other. He had a way of handling sheep that I have never seen anyone else use. Instead of using the flat of his hand he used his clenched fist to feel up their backs.

Alas, like so many more, these two great characters are no longer with us, but thinking of them reminded me of a verse by Rudyard Kipling:

His dead are in the churchyard thirty generations laid.
Their names went down in Domesday Book when
  Domesday Book was made;
And the passion and the piety and prowess of his line
Have seeded, rooted, fruited in some land the Law calls
  mine.

In 1974, I was elected to the Breed Council and two years later to the Judges' Panel. David followed me onto the Council in 1983 and two years later he also became a Judge. To achieve something you have always dreamed about is gratifying, but when your son follows in your footsteps it is doubly so. In 1986, the Society selected me as their President. If anyone had told me in 1968 when we went to Chidham to purchase our first ewes that I would one day become President of the Society, I would have laughed at them. Even today, when I look through the list of past presidents, containing so many illustrious names who have held office over the last hundred years (including a dozen peers of the realm) I am rather awed to see my name added to that list. Then I feel rather proud, for I am the first person to come up through the ranks from Shepherd to President – and to be Shepherd and President at the same time.

Shows and Sales

SHOWING is somewhat like smoking: once you start you tend to get addicted. I started some forty years ago and it has been a part of my life ever since. I have derived a great deal of pleasure from it and over the years have made a host of friends and met many charming people.

The shows can be divided into two categories: the local, one-day shows which are great fun but about which no one gets excited; and the two- to four-day county and national shows for which competitors often travel long distances. The climax of the summer shows is, of course, the Royal of England. That is where we sort out the men from the boys. Similarly, the Royal Smithfield is the highlight of the Christmas season.

The actual showing is the result of a whole year's work – a year of working seven days a week, often in adverse weather conditions. But one tends to forget all the trials and tribulations when arriving for the first show of the season and meeting old friends and competitors. I would stress that most are both friends *and* competitors. There has always been a great comradeship in the sheep lines and if anyone is in trouble, he will always get help. When in the ring, however, it is every man for himself and you do anything in your power to win within the rules. Occasionally you bend them slightly, but once the cards and rosettes have been given out you are the best of friends again. The time-honoured handshake from the second man in the line to the winner confirms this.

There was, and still is, something special about arriving at the first show of the season – meeting friends and competitors (who in many cases you had not seen since the last ram sales the previous autumn), looking at what their sheep were like and assessing your own chances against them. In spite of the competition, there was always a great spirit of comradeship among the shepherds. We worked, slept and ate together and if anyone had trouble we all rallied round to help them out. In the ring, we did everything in our power to win and the others did the same, but we always remained the best of friends.

Two major changes have taken place in the last twenty years. First, all the major shows including the Royal have moved to permanent sites, which has resulted in greatly improved amenities for competitors, animals and the public. We now have permanent roads, drainage, eating, sleeping and toilet facilities and much better accommodation for the animals. The other major change has been the almost total demise of the large, pedigree ram breeding flocks with their professional shepherds. Most of today's pedigree flocks are comparatively small and are shepherded by their owners. This is a change that has been brought about entirely by economic pressure. Twenty years ago a good ram lamb would pay the shepherd's wages for six weeks. Today it would not be enough for two.

Transport has changed greatly. Nowadays most exhibitors of livestock have their own lorries or boxes and, of course, the road network has improved. When I first started there were no motorways and the lorries had a speed limit of thirty miles per hour. In those days, it was quite an adventure setting off on a two hundred mile journey. I well remember the last travelling Royal (in 1962) at Newcastle – a journey of some four hundred miles from Somerset. Three of us, with a lorry each, drove up in convoy. We had a burst tyre, were the first on the scene of a nasty accident, filled one of the lorries with diesel instead of petrol, got lost going through Leicester and finished up outside the cemetery at one o'clock in the morning. On reaching Newcastle early next morning, we found all the canvas over the sheep lines had blown away in an overnight gale. Those were the days before tacographs.

In all our travels I was only once pulled in by the police, going out of Lechlade on the way to the Royal. Before leaving home we had screwed back the injectors to make the old Commer pull better. She was just about pushing out the smoke when a police car waved me in. The officer had a good look round, checked the licence and asked to see the log book. I had one, but the last entry had been over two years before. I put on the country yokel act, looking simple and pleading ignorance. He then asked if I had a heavy goods licence. "I've got one of they, officer," I replied in my best Dorset dialect, digging it out from my inside coat pocket as proud as punch. He took one look and shook his head in disbelief. I'd had the damn thing for two years and had forgotten to sign it. I gave him a second helping of the simple countryman and was told to fill in the log book, sign the licence and get the hell out of it. Off he went, forgetting all about the smoke. I never had an accident, but did, on one occasion, knock over a diesel pump when backing up. I still think someone must have moved it!

The worst journey I can remember was returning home from Smithfield in 1962 in the smog. Visibility, by mid-afternoon, was down to a couple of yards and we were over four hours getting to Staines. We crept slowly along following the cats' eyes until we came to a large roundabout. A policeman with a torch waved us down and enquired where we thought we were going. "West, officer," I replied.

"Well, you have been past me twice," he grinned. He

put us on the right road, the smog suddenly disappeared and we drove home in beautiful moonlight.

We always travelled to the major shows a day or two before judging to allow the sheep time to settle in and look their best on the day. Most shows now have quite good sleeping accommodation for exhibitors, but a great many people still sleep and eat in their lorries. For many years, when we had from ten to sixteen shepherds out at every show in the Dorset Downs, we used to park three lorries side by side, sleeping in the two outside ones and eating in the centre one. With deck boards on top of straw bales down the centre forming a table and more straw bales down either side providing the seats, this was our dining room. The lorries used for sleeping in were sheeted over the top and sides with a rick sheet to keep out the draught and any rain. The floor was covered with a thick layer of straw to form a mattress and sleeping bags on top made it quite a comfortable dormitory. Primus stoves were then the most popular means of cooking and tea making, but we were quite modern for the times and between us had two double-burner Calor gas stoves. This must have created quite a fire risk but I can never remember an incident. Cooking for up to sixteen was quite a performance. I was generally one of the cooks, not because of my ability, but because the cook was not expected to wash up. Another reason was that I did not smoke and no one approved of cigarette ash in the frying pan!

Each morning, the sheep were first cleaned out, bedded up and fed, filling them up for the day. Then we had a good breakfast at about seven-thirty. We used two double gas burners with four frying-pans, one each for eggs, bacon, sausages and fried bread. As the food was cooked, it was put on the table and the cook kept going until everyone stopped eating. We generally had another cooked meal in the evening. Several of the flock masters did a bit of market gardening and early potato growing, so that at most shows after the middle of June, there would be several bags of peas, beans and potatoes that had been acquired. These, with cold meat or spit-roasted chicken (which we could buy at the showground) followed by tinned fruit and custard, made up our evening meal. Both meals were washed down by what seemed like gallons of tea.

Most of the trimming had been done at home prior to departure but a final tidy-up always took place before judging, for presentation is half the art of winning and selling. Judging mornings are always hectic. You are up early to feed and clean out your sheep, have breakfast, wash, shave and change. The shepherd, as well as the sheep, has to look smart – a final touch-up and at nine to nine-thirty judging starts. Formerly we were judged in the lines, but now most shows have rings – a great improvement for both competitors and the public. Over the years I have known a great many judges, most of whom were very good and knew their job. What must always be remembered is that the judge has been asked to pass his opinion on the animal before him and it is his opinion and decision that counts on the day. He cannot please everyone and if he has any sense he will please himself. I always reckon you can tell what sort of a judge you have when he comes to judge his champion. If he has five or six first prizewinners that are all of the same type then he has done his job properly. It makes no difference whether you like that particular type or not. It is his day and he has gone for what he likes.

After judging, it is traditional for the winner to take all the competitors and their shepherds to the bar for a drink. Such parties have a habit of going on for some time. I can remember on many occasions going to the bar about midday and leaving in time to feed up in the evening. But it was an unwritten law that no one drank the evening before judging. A year or two ago a young lady won at Smithfield for the first time and after being congratulated by the other competitors, was told: "Now my dear, you are going to learn what it means to pay for success." There were, and still are, some great characters in the show world and I have been lucky enough to know many of them. They worked hard and played hard and enjoyed themselves.

The late Ted Frampton was one of these. A legend in his own lifetime, he won the Supreme Champion at Royal Smithfield on many occasions. He was a tall, raw-boned man with a very forthright manner. If he thought you were a bloody fool, he told you so without wrapping it up. To see him the day before judging, in a shirt open to the waist and wearing an old pair of carpet slippers, he looked almost like a tramp; but on judging morning, or when going out in the evening dressed in a smart dark suit with a flower in his buttonhole, he looked, and was, a gentleman. Ted never wasted words. The first time Texel sheep were exhibited at Smithfield they were short – and many still are. When asked his opinion, Ted took a long, hard look. "Them's breath smells," he snapped. On being asked what he meant, he replied: "Their heads be too near their arses." On his retirement, we took up a collection among the shepherds and stewards at Smithfield and he was presented with an engraved silver half-hunter watch by Princess Anne. He knew nothing of what was afoot, only that he was going to be presented to Her Royal Highness in the sheep ring. It was my job to get him there at the proper time. We were standing in the far corner as Princess Anne arrived, dressed in a very smart tweed costume. Ted eyed up the situation and out came another of his famous remarks: "Sire, she ain't arf horsey."

The year the Royal Counties took place at Poole, Mr

Stewart Tory was the Hampshire Down judge. I got up at about five o'clock and had a quick look around the Dorset Down sheep while the kettle was boiling for tea. It was a beautiful June morning, the sun just coming up, not a cloud to be seen, and as I returned to the lorry Ted was going up to see his sheep.

"Morning, Ted; grand morning," I greeted him.

"Morning boy, 'tis a grand morning 'til Stewart do come and spoil her," he replied. He was, without doubt, one of the great shepherds of his day and Smithfield never seems the same without him.

Many amusing incidents take place on the showground. At the first Royal at Stoneleigh it had been raining for several days and the entire field was covered with a two-inch layer of sloppy mud. We had been to the Annual Dinner given by Coopers for the stockmen and shepherds. As we came out it was still raining and about a dozen of us piled into a Land Rover to ride back to the lines. Frank Radford was the last on and as he sat down on the tailboard Michael Flatt, who was driving, let in the clutch, gave her some wellie and shot off like a bullet, leaving Frank face down in the mud. We got him back to our lorries and had to hose the mud off his clothes. A couple of years later, Fred Dunford had a "session" and about mid-day sat down under a newly planted tree and went to sleep. Unfortunately, we had the father and mother of a thunderstorm which he slept through, waking up to find himself wet through to the skin.

The same year George Penny slipped down the ramp of his lorry one evening and injured his back. We got him up to the Red Cross tent where the doctor gave him a pain-killing injection and promised to send someone down first thing in the morning to see how he was. Early next day, George was taken a cup of tea in bed; and a rather splendid pot plant suddenly appeared, having been acquired from some unfortunate stand holder. About half a dozen of us were in the lorry when a very motherly Red Cross nurse appeared, enquired how George was and accepted a cup of tea. Looking around the company present she remarked: "What a wonderful lot of friends you have. They've given you tea in bed and even brought flowers to cheer you up." This brought the rejoinder from the gentleman who had obtained the plant: "We ain't brought they to cheer him up, my dear, they's for the funeral 'safernoon."

Yeovil Show in the late fifties and early sixties was one of the biggest and best one-day shows in the south-west. It was a particular favourite of Arthur Whittle, a shepherd of the old school. He worshipped his sheep, especially the ewes; and as Yeovil had special breeding ewe classes for pairs of two teeth, four teeth and six teeth Dorset Downs, he could exhibit his pride and joy. In 1965 Newburgh had a grand team of ewes out, with Hughie Cannon judging; he was a rather corpulent gentleman with a round, red face and really looked what he was – a farmer. On this particular occasion, Hughie was very much below par and still suffering a hangover from the night before, which was not unusual for him. We won the two teeth class without too much trouble, then took out a grand pen of four teeth. Hughie came down the line and after handling them, muttered to Arthur: "Wonderful pen of sheep, Shep." We thought that we had that one in the bag – like hell we did, for at the last moment we were put down into second place. Arthur was not amused. Then we went out with the sixes and by this time the sun was blazing down and Hughie was visibly wilting. We were standing at the top of the line with our ewes, with a pair of very coarse, black-headed sheep in second place. After fiddling around for quite a while Hughie told us to change round, putting the dark ewes first and ours second. As we moved down into second place Arthur looked him straight in the eye, muttering: "Go and drown your bloody self." Hughie gathered himself together, took another look, then turned back to Arthur. "Sorry, Shep, put 'em back how they were." We won the class and went on to win the championship.

At Newburgh we used to show at about five major shows between early May and the beginning of July, the last being the Royal of England. The shows were all spaced out so that there was a clear week between each one: these were very busy times indeed as, besides having the regular work to do, the show team was constantly being changed. We usually arrived home on Saturday evening after a show and on Sunday morning, while having breakfast in the sheep house, a post mortem was held on the successes and failures of the previous week and plans were made for the next time out. First of all the judge: his known likes and dislikes were discussed and taken into account, then an assessment of the team was made. Would they stand another show without going over the top? Any that had not been in the running were almost always discarded and fresh ones brought in. Occasionally a winner was left out if we had, or thought we had, a better one. Sheep that had been really fit for, say, the Devon County or Bath and West would invariably be over the top by the Royal. Billy Boss was generally late for his own breakfast on these mornings. The upshot of all this was that several fresh sheep had to be trimmed from scratch and matched up. By the time this was done to everyone's satisfaction, we were off again.

On the Thursday after the Royal, the Dorset Down Sheep Breeders held their annual July Show and Sale at Dorchester. There was a class for draft ewes and several classes for rams: single ram lambs, pairs of ram lambs, pen of three ram lambs, and shearling rams, each member being restricted to an entry of seven rams. On one occasion, we

144

won the single and pen of three ram lambs and were second with the pair.

Besides the rams, we used to take seventy to eighty regular draft ewes and about twenty-five shearlings, all of which had been trimmed for sale. This was one of the most important days of our year and there was great rivalry for the top price and top average. The ewes were sold in the fair field in bunches of from ten to fifty. In Mr Tom's time, when the flock was six hundred strong, Newburgh had always sold the best draft ewes in a straight hundred. They were, I believe, the last Dorset Down flock to do so. In my time we still sold the top pen of fifty.

The rams were sold in the market and the moment of truth for each breeder came when it was their turn to sell. The strawed-up ring had lines of tiered seats around it, with Major John or Major Oliver Duke in the box. The seats were filled with breeders and prospective buyers. In we went with the pick of the sheep we had bred that season. A year's work had gone into producing them and now the result of these efforts was going to be assessed by some of the best sheep men in the country. To stand in front of my fellow professionals with a run of sheep of which I am justly proud is one of the things in life that always gives me a great thrill and sense of achievement. You had selected the ewes for mating and lambed them, reared the lambs and turned them out; they are all your own work and they reflect your skill as a shepherd. In all the years I have been in the game only once have I gone to a Breed Show and Sale with rams of which I was not proud and on that occasion I had taken on a flock with the ewes already in lamb, so I'd had no hand in the breeding of the lamb crop. By the next year I had put that right – but that is another story.

The stud rams were put out with the ewes the same week as the Show and Sale. The flock was split into bunches of about fifty, each with a ram. As far as possible, we used to divide them into families; all the ewes sired by the same ram were in one bunch. There were always about a dozen stock rams, including several of our own breeding. Each year we bought two or three at the Show and Sale, trying them on just a few ewes the first time round. If their progeny did not come up to expectations they were sold on the next year as shearlings. This used to be the case with about half the rams bought.

After the July sale there was a short breathing space before the commercial ram selling began properly. During this time, as many rams as possible were backed out and trimmed over once up in the field. This eased the workload when the sales started in earnest. When they did, we had well over a hundred rams to trim, take out and sell in about six weeks. A few were sold at home but the majority were taken to fairs across the south of England: Axminster, Newton Abbot, South Molton and Barnstaple in Devon to the west; Ashford, Maidstone, Lewes and Findon to the east; up country to Reading, Bicester, Gloucester and Hereford. This involved a lot of travelling, but we used to journey there, sell the rams and return the same day – even to Ashford and Hereford. Of course, there were no motorways then, nor the Severn Bridge. The Kent trips meant leaving home by four o'clock in the morning and not getting back until late evening. The next morning we were on parade at the fold by seven o'clock. In those days I was young and fit and, I think now, just a little crazy. No matter how early we loaded up Billy Boss was always there to help and, as we climbed in the lorry, he produced from his back pocket a ten shilling note, screwed up in a tiny ball. Fifty pence does not seem much today, but in those days you could get a good meal in a transport café for three or four shillings.

By mid-morning the customers began to arrive, having

decided what breed they were looking for. After walking round all the rams of their chosen breed, they would go into the pens and handle the ones they liked best, marking their catalogues as they went. They invariably bought the rams they had selected and when they came into the ring, would bid to a standard and not to a price. Nowadays you see very few buyers around the rams prior to auction. They tend to stand around the ring, waiting until something comes in that they like the look of which is at a price they can afford, and buy it. At, say, two hundred they like the sheep, but at two fifty they seem to take a sudden dislike to it!

For me the selling part of the job was, and is, like the sight of hounds to the hunter. I love the good-natured banter and leg pulling that goes on at the sales both outside and inside the ring. Selling in the West Country, especially in Devon, was completely different from that further east, both in the type of men one dealt with and the size of the business they ran. The whole speed of life was so much slower in the west. No one ever seemed to be in any hurry – not even the auctioneers. A buyer would wander around and, after a while, pick out a ram he fancied, then he would send the boy (they always seemed to have a lad with them) to fetch "Uncle George" or "Grandad", who on his arrival would pass his opinion. This was a very serious business and not to be hurried in any way. They were also very thrifty and were quite prepared to haggle all day over a pound. If the ram they fancied had not reached its reserve at auction they would follow us back to the pens and then protracted negotiation would take place as they tried to get the price reduced. Sometimes the deal was struck on condition that you delivered the ram on your way home. The trouble with this, very often, was finding the farm! There were miles of narrow lanes, all with high banks topped with beech hedges, and very narrow gateways with stone posts. You could go for miles to find a place to turn the lorry if you went wrong. The great advantage was that after delivering the ram you were always assured of a good tea before you set off for home.

The Devon farmers were only excelled in their thriftiness by the men from the Welsh Border Country. They were as tight as a duck's arse under water – and that is water-tight! I remember one day in Hereford market, when there had been quite a lot of interest in the rams before we went into the ring but only one was sold at the reserve price of thirty-eight guineas. Several farmers followed the rams back to the pens and messed about, trying to buy at a reduced price. After about an hour of this nonsense I got a bit short with them, backed the lorry in and started to load. Within a short time I'd sold all but one ram at the reserve price. One old farmer, who had been trying to beat me down all day, offered thirty-five for this ram. I refused and loaded him up, had a cup of tea and then started to drive out of the market. Glancing in the mirror as I pulled away, I spotted the old boy waving at me to stop. He came up and said that he had decided to buy the ram after all. I thanked him for his custom but told him the price was now forty guineas. He exploded: "You offered him to me for thirty-eight not ten minutes ago," he yelled.

"I know that, but it cost a pound to put the tailboard up and another to pull her down," I retorted. Then to my amazement, and with a lot of bad language, he agreed to buy for forty guineas – my top price of the day.

The Kent and Findon trade was completely different. The much larger farms of the South Downs and Romney Marsh often carried flocks of over a thousand ewes. These farmers would very often buy eight or ten rams at a time. The marsh men from Kent used to prefer shearlings to ram lambs. Indeed, they would pay more for second class shearlings than first class lambs. The cold, wet conditions of Romney Marsh were, in many cases, too severe for lambs to survive. The sales here were held later in the year than in the West Country, Findon being the first on the second Saturday in September. The Ashford sales did not start until the first week in October and continued until the first week in November, as the traditional time for turning out rams on Romney Marsh was November 5th. Many farmers would not buy their rams until it was time to put them out.

Unlike the summer shows, where breeding animals are exhibited, Smithfield is a fatstock show entirely for butchers' animals. There are classes for pure breds, butchers' weight classes for both pure and crossbreds, and carcase competitions.

We would travel up on Friday, judging took place on Sunday afternoon and Monday and we returned home when the show closed the following Friday. Saturday and Sunday were always spent trimming. After getting our own sheep ready, there always seemed to be a number of exhibitors looking for someone to trim their sheep for them. We generally reckoned to make a bit of spending money on Sunday. We were, and still are, accommodated in a large hall (Richmond Hall), three storeys up at Earls Court. Beds and mattresses are provided and there are also cooking and washing facilities. The shepherds sleep on one side of the hall and the pigmen on the other. We cook our own breakfast, have a snack lunch and generally go out for a meal in the evening, but we always find that things tend to be much more expensive in London than at home, especially if we buy food inside Earls Court. I well remember one year, when judging did not finish until after three o'clock and we had not eaten since breakfast at seven-thirty. We decided to have a drink and George Payne, spotting some beef sandwiches behind the bar, called for two rounds. The barmaid served him and asked for one pound eighty pence. George nearly exploded: "One pound eighty be damned. 'Twould be cheaper to go downstairs and buy a bloody bullock," he snorted. He didn't really enjoy those sandwiches.

The first time Bill Webb won the Prince of Wales Cup, he and George went out in the evening to fetch two or three bottles of whisky for a celebration in Richmond Hall. They partook rather heavily on the way back and arrived a little under the weather. The doors into Richmond Hall are fitted with springs to keep them closed. George gave the door an almighty push and kept walking, but looked back over his shoulder to see where Bill was. The door flew open and the spring forced it to close just as quickly, catching him on the side of the face and knocking him out cold. We brought him round, put him on his bed, and agreed amongst ourselves that between the whisky and the door he was due for a hell of a bad head in the morning. Brian Dibben disagreed and reckoned he had some pills that would put him right.

"But how are you going to get them into him?" I enquired, looking at George flat out asleep on the bed.

"Simple," replied Dibby. "Just hold his nose and stuff 'em in." He fetched the pills and we all crowded round to see fair play. Dibby grabbed hold of George's nose (there is a fair bit of it) and his mouth opened to reveal two long, fang-like teeth in front and a mouthful of stumps. Dibby took a long look and shook his head. "I ain't putting my fingers in there – no-how." George did not get his pills and in the morning he had a head like a bushel basket.

On another occasion, when returning to Richmond Hall in the early hours three sheets to the wind, George, Arthur Vaughan and my son David decided to wake up the pigmen. They ran out the fire hose, got Arthur on the end, then twisted open all the valves they could find. To no avail – no water came through. At one stage, Arthur was sitting on a bed holding the fire hose out in front at arm's length so that he could see down the pipe, muttering: "The damn thing's gone dry." After a while they got tired of messing about and went to bed. The next morning the hose was where they had left it, but when we tried the valves again the water shot out. I dread to think what would have happened if it had worked a few hours earlier!

One year Fred Dunford sent his lambs up to the Smithfield but did not come himself. We found out why on Monday morning. As his sheep were being judged, one of them started to lamb in the ring and about an hour later produced a fine ram lamb in the sheep hospital. Now this was too good an incident to let pass unnoticed. You just don't have in-lamb sheep at a fat stock show, let alone one giving birth. As we were going to bed that night, we decided to send Fred a telegram and after much thought concocted the following:

FREDERICK DUNFORD, SHEPHERD EXTRAORDINARY, WOOL, DORSET.
CONGRATULATIONS. IT'S A BOY.

We 'phoned it through and the young lady on the switchboard suggested that we send a special greetings telegram which would cost a further forty pence. (She thought it was really a boy.) Another four ten pence pieces went in and we were assured that it would be delivered by first post in the morning. We insisted that we wanted it delivered straight away, which cost another sixty pence. By that time we were running out of ten pence pieces, but managed to rustle up the extra. Back at the farm, Fred had returned from the lambing pens at midnight and gone to bed, only to be awakened by the telegraph boy at 1:30 a.m.!

For my sins, I am now a judge and I sometimes feel rather like the poacher who turned gamekeeper. The first

Breed Society to put me on their panel was the Jacobs. I was button-holed by Lady Aldington, their Chairman at the time. Anyone who has met her will know she is a lady of great presence. Quite out of the blue, she said: "John, I want you to become a Jacob judge." I pointed out to her that I had never kept Jacob sheep and that it was most unlikely I ever would. She brushed away my excuses with a wave of her hand. "You don't keep Jacobs but you *do* know sheep." I could see no future in trying to be an immovable object in the path of an irresistible force. I gracefully accepted and it has brought me a great deal of pleasure and enjoyment over the years.

Most exhibitors accept the judge's decision with good grace, but there is the occasional awkward one. The trouble with so many of these people is not so much that they don't know, but that they don't know they don't know. Then there are the clever ones who try to bend the rules. These are the ones I love to catch out. I have tried all these dodges myself at one time or another and can generally recognise what they are up to. There is a lot in the old saying: "It takes a rogue to catch one." Another little ploy is to tell the judge that the sheep they are holding have already won at some previous show. The first time that I judged Southdowns was the Kent Show. While talking to another breeder, he mentioned that it was my first time with Southdowns and wished me luck and hoped that I would enjoy doing it. I thanked him and assured him that I was certain I would enjoy myself. Looking a little puzzled, he enquired why, to which I replied: "For the last twenty years, you chaps have been messing me about and now it is my turn to mess you about." But the language I used was somewhat stronger!

The ultimate in judging, as in showing, is the Royal Show and I was very proud to be asked to judge the Southdown classes in 1986. It was a day that I shall never forget.

Piddlehinton

EAST Farm, Piddlehinton, some five miles north of
Dorchester, was a smaller edition of Newburgh. It was
situated on both sides of the village which straggles alongside the River Piddle, the land sloping gently away on
both sides of the river to Dules Wood in the east and
almost up to the old Sherborne Road in the west. A dairy
was milked on the west side and most of the arable, where
the sheep were kept, was situated on the east side. The
farm had been in the hands of the Lovelace family since
1840 and a flock of Dorset Downs had been kept there
since that time. They, like the Newburgh flock, were in
the first edition of the Flock Book.

Rex Lovelace was a man very much in the mould of
Billy Boss. His father had died during the Depression of
the late 1920s and Rex, or Farmer, as everyone, including
his wife, called him, had taken on the management of the
farm when he was only nineteen. Those early years in
business had left their mark. He was as straight as a gun
barrel but as keen as mustard, especially where money was
concerned.

He had a grand flock of big, strong if somewhat dark
sheep, but for several years had been having shepherd
trouble and the flock had gone downhill somewhat. I had
been working in Kent for about four years and met Rex at
Findon, where I was ram buying. Over a drink after the
auction, I let it slip that I was not too happy and he offered
me his flock.

A couple of weeks later we went to Dorset to have a look. The ewes had gone back a bit since I had last seen them, some five years before, and quite a lot of ram lambs remained unsold. These lambs were not very clever, in spite of being in a good piece of kale. There were two good fields of swedes and kale, plenty of good hay and the vetches were up strong. The grub situation here looked all right, I thought, so I went into the sheep house to have a look at the trough grub they were feeding on. It was a mixture of oats, linseed cake, peas and flaked maize – a mixture that I had always been used to. As I came out of the sheep house and down the steps, Rex was sitting on the tailgate of the Land Rover, puffing at his beloved pipe.

"What do you think?" he asked.

"Only one thing wrong here," I said. "The grub's been the wrong side of the hurdles for too long."

We drove on up to the brick and flint shepherd's cottage, with a yard and a set of buildings behind it, situated half way between the village and Dules Wood. It was right in the middle of the land on which the sheep were kept. A few alterations to the cottage were agreed without too much fuss and we went down to the farmhouse for lunch. Afterwards we got down to talking money. The lambing, shearing and ram bonuses were agreed without any trouble, then came the crunch. Rex filled the glasses. "Now, Shep, how much a week?" This, remember, was 1972. I was agreeing to shepherd three hundred Dorset Down ewes plus ewe tegs and bring out one hundred rams with only part-time help, working seven days a week with two weeks' holiday a year.

I took a sip of whisky. "Can't be done under fifteen pounds a week."

Rex flung up his arms in horror. "I can't do it, Shep. I'd like to, but it just ain't possible."

I wondered if I had over-done it, then remembered

what Arthur once told me. "Never sell yourself short. If they wants you bad enough, they'll pay." We argued for some time. Rex had crept up to fourteen pounds. Stalemate had been reached, so he changed the subject. "Going back tonight?" he asked.

"All according if we agree. If not, I shall stay over and look at a Hampshire flock on the way back" (there were two Hampshire breeders advertising at the time).

"Hell," grunted Rex, "fourteen ten."

"No, shan't deal under fifteen." I was sensing victory.

A few more deep puffs at his pipe, then he stood up and extended his hand: "Fifteen it is then, Shep." We shook on the deal and that was it. No contract of employment, no agreement to sign; his word was good enough for me, mine for him. He refilled the glasses and we drank to the future. Putting down his glass, he asked, "Which of they Hamp flocks were you going to see?"

"Neither," I grinned.

"Didn't think you bloody well were," came the reply.

The basic rotation was the same as at Newburgh regarding crops grown for the sheep. There were a few minor differences in the management, several of which made life a little easier. The central situation of the cottage and building meant that the sheep were never more than half a mile from home. The ewes were lambed in a permanent building within fifty yards of the cottage and in the summer, when folding grass, electrified netting was used in place of wire netting and hurdles. This was a lot easier and quicker to erect and much lighter to carry than conventional wire netting.

We moved back to Dorset on a Thursday in mid-October, the intention being to start work on the following Monday. The previous shepherd had left some five or six weeks previously. Rex, assisted by old George, had been looking after the sheep in the meantime. The ram lambs were still in the kale, the hoggets running grass and the ewes were folded on grass, or rather they were supposed to be. They were breaking out as fast as they were put in. Rex came along Friday mid-morning. "For God's sake come up and give a hand. They ewes be driving I mad. Can't keep them in no-how." Up we went to find the flock all over a twenty-acre field. Some had gone through the hedge into an adjoining field of roots, not for the first time, as quite a patch had been eaten off. The dogs fetched them out and they were put into a stubble field until things could be sorted out.

George went off and cut a load of new shores which were pointed and nailed that day, and on Saturday I went up and pitched out a square fold measuring fifty yards by fifty yards (roughly half an acre), using all new shores spaced at three-yard intervals. Sunday morning came and the damn things were all out again; they had not managed to snap the shores this time but had pulled the wire down from the top nails. They were put back and the next fold pitched out with shores every two yards. They behaved until first light on Monday morning, when they started to create hell with their bleating. I went straight up as soon as I heard them, to find about a dozen over the wire and the rest running up and down trying to follow them out. Again the wire netting had been pulled off the top nails on several shores, allowing it to sag. Back they went yet again and were let on into the next fold. Returning at about ten o'clock, I caught two of the ring-leaders getting out again. They were walking up the wire with their front legs, as if they were climbing a ladder. As soon as their feet were over the top strand they leaned forward, pulling the wire off the nails, and with a bound they were over. They were what was known as "wire climbers".

I have never been a trial man, but have always had good working dogs and several of them. The pack I had at that time were no exception. For the last four years they had been working a thousand Kent ewes on Romney Marsh, so Down ewes were child's play for them. They could, on occasion, be quick and, if encouraged, a bit rough. As I walked in through the gate, I was greeted by the sight of the two ewes climbing up and springing over the wire. The second they were over I put the dogs round them. They raced them up and down the wire until they lay down utterly exhausted and frightened to death. Back in the fold they stood panting, with their heads almost touching the ground – a picture of absolute dejection.

Then Farmer descended on me like the wrath of the gods and we had our first and only stand-up row. Of course, we had our arguments and disagreements at other times, but this was the only time we had a real slanging match. They were sowing wheat a couple of fields away and Rex had witnessed the little episode. Down came the Land Rover like a bat out of hell. "What the devil do you think you are doing, Shepherd?" he yelled. "They ewes be half way in-lamb. I ain't having this carry on."

Now I had been trying to keep these sheep in all weekend and it had not improved my rather quick temper when they persisted in getting the better of me. Rex's intervention was the straw that broke the camel's back:

"Who the hell do you think you are shouting at?" I roared. "You didn't tell me you had a flock of blasted riggers. Your last shepherd could not keep 'em in, neither could you. Well, I damn well am, one way or t'other. You got a shepherd now, not a bloody labourer."

We glared at each other for several minutes without speaking. Rex's pipe expelled smoke rings like Red Indian war signals, then they slowly ceased as he removed it from his mouth. "I am sorry, Shep. I forgot me manners. 'Tis a long time since I had a proper shepherd. I'll wish 'ee a good day and leave 'ee to it." With that, he was gone and the incident was never mentioned again.

Several times during that morning ewes tried to get over the wire. Each time, the dogs were there to drive them back and after a while they began to settle down to eating what they had and not looking to get out for more. They were not getting out because they were hungry; it was just a habit they had been allowed to get into, a habit that no good hurdled shepherd would tolerate. For the next few days I almost lived with the ewes and every time I caught one trying the wire she had the dogs onto her. By this method, and by setting the wire up very carefully, we overcame the problem. The whole success of this method was to catch the offenders in the act. It was no good dogging them when they had been out for ten minutes.

The building used for lambing was a large, lean-to structure on the back of the old barn. The couple and nursery pens were erected in the barn itself and there was a communicating door between the two buildings. A yard in front of the lean-to shed was used to corn and hay the ewes in, before turning them out into a fold of grass after breakfast. They were returned to the lambing shed in the early afternoon. As they lambed, they were put into coops for the first day or two, then on into the nursery pens for a few days, before being turned out onto the grass. This is one of the snags encountered when using permanent lambing yards. It is often not possible to let the ewes and lambs out by day and back by night because the grub is generally some distance away. This means that the baby lambs and their mothers have to stay in the nursery pens until they are strong enough to stand the weather. When it's wet this can often be a week or more. We used to use long canvas sheets, some twenty yards long by a yard high, which were tied onto the hurdles to make a wind-break for the young lambs.

There are, of course, many advantages with a permanent

yard. First, it takes a lot less time and effort to get ready for lambing, with no yard to build. One of the greatest improvements is mains electricity: no more going around with a Tilly lantern or torch. Now, at the press of a button, the whole shed is brilliantly lit and both your hands are free to catch or hold a sheep without the worry of the lantern being knocked over and causing a fire. At Piddle-hinton, as the cottage was so close to the lambing yard, the sheep house was dispensed with. It was so much more comfortable to go indoors and sit by the fire for a couple of hours than to stay in the hut.

The whole concept of permanent lambing yards has been made practicable by the introduction of preventive medicine. Before the advent of clostridial vaccines it was courting disaster to lamb repeatedly in the same place, hence the use of temporary yards which were moved annually. The two most prevalent diseases were lamb dysentery and tetanus. These, with several others, can now be controlled with a single injection given to the ewes a month prior to lambing, the immunity being passed on to the lambs by the ewes' milk. Until we had this simple and inexpensive system, very few lambs recovered after contracting either of these complaints.

Like Billy Boss, Rex always put in an appearance before breakfast, and at lambing time he used to come up again most days and turn out the ewes and lambs from the nursery pens and up the farm track to the field, where they had plenty of grass. Some years, this was half a mile away. Off he would go with half a dozen couples and slowly and gently walk them away up the track, wandering along behind them, puffing away at his beloved pipe.

Tailing was carried out in very much the same way as at Newburgh, the main difference being that Rex always held the lambs himself and as soon as we had finished the tails were counted. Picking up a piece of chalk and using the tailing stool as a blackboard, we would work out the lambing bonus, which was one shilling per tail up to the number of ewes, plus two shillings per tail for every tail over that number. The bonus amounted to between twenty and twenty-five pounds. He then pulled out his wallet and paid up there and then. Paying the lambing bonus in the field as soon as tailing was completed was a tradition he had inherited from his father. I well remember the first time we tailed: the bonus came to twenty-three pounds, nineteen shillings. Rex gave me twenty-four one pound notes and asked for a shilling change!

One Saturday in late May we drove off to Devon to look at a bunch of shearling rams that were for sale. I picked up Rex outside his home at Glebe House just before twelve on a beautiful, early summer's day. As he climbed into the lorry, I enquired if he had the farm address. "Burnards, Holsworthy," came the reply. I reminded him that there were a lot of Burnards down there and Holsworthy was quite a large area. Back into the house he went, to return a few moments later with the Flock Book containing the address and a new tin of tobacco. "Good job you sent I back, Shep. I'd forgot my baccy," he said as he settled into his seat and proceeded to empty the tin of tobacco into his pouch.

To go on a trip like this with Rex Lovelace was an education in itself. He would sit in the passenger seat, get his pipe going to his satisfaction and then proceed to "farm" both sides of the road as we went along, his eyes missing nothing. A good piece of corn, mowing grass or roots were duly noted, and if we were within forty miles of home he generally knew the farmer concerned. On one trip to Wilton, we passed a piece of wheat with a lot of poppy showing red in the corn. "Never seen red weed there before," he grunted. "I'll rub that into Jack next time I sees him." Livestock always attracted his attention. We would be driving along quite merrily when suddenly he would spot a good dairy of cows, a bunch of young stock or a flock of sheep. "Here, steady up, Shep, just look at that bunch of in-calvers. Ain't they a picture?"

This was the mood he was in as we set off that summer morning. Leaving Dorchester, we headed due west over the rolling downland of West Dorset onto the top of the ridge above Askerswell, with a view over the Bride Valley to the sea at West Bay on our left and away to the ridge at Rampisham on the right; down into and through Bridport, famous for its rope and net making, with its wide streets and even wider pavements. On into the hillier country beyond and down into Chideock, Charmouth and the market town of Axminster, changing gear all the time, with Rex's running commentary on the crops and stock as we went. The good were praised, the poor tut-tutted at and the run-of-the-mill passed without comment.

After Axminster, we reached Devon proper, with that lovely, red soil. "Grow anything and fat a gate-post" was Rex's comment. Devon is a county of smaller farms and fields than Dorset with, in those days, a lot of beef cattle and sheep as well as dairy cows and much less arable than there is now. Then through Honiton and round the old Exeter bypass in the same sort of country and on to Okehampton, skirting along the north side of Dartmoor, into much harder country. "Best crop this ground grows is stones," said Rex when we stopped to stretch our legs and have a cup of tea. Then it was on to Hatherleigh and our destination at Holsworthy in much better country, but nothing like the Honiton–Exeter area.

The rams we had come to see were penned in a yard ready for inspection. They were big-framed shearlings, but on the poor side because the owner had failed to sell them the previous autumn as ram lambs. We walked through them slowly, summing them up. They had only just been shorn and not very well at that, which made them look even worse than they really were. "If we can buy 'em half sensible, hang some meat onto 'em in the next three or four months, I reckon they could pay a bob or two" was Rex's summing up.

He then proceeded to show me how to buy things "half sensible", as he put it. He walked over to the owner, who was standing by the yard gate slowly puffing at his pipe and seemingly deep in thought. "Well, young man, they be on the poor side. Pity you had not done them better last winter, but I ain't here to throw stones at 'em. Now I'll tell 'ee what I'll do; I'll bid 'ee once and once only. I'll take the lot as they stand at fifty-five a piece. Now choose now and choose quick, 'cause we got a long way to go home."

The owner looked worried: "But some of them is worth a lot more than that," he protested.

"So they may be, but I bid 'ee for the lot, not the best and I ain't going horse dealing." Rex pulled his cheque book out. "Well, do I make it out or do we go home without em?" he asked. They shook hands and that was that. We loaded up, had a cup of tea and started for home.

"That was a bit sharp," I suggested, when we had regained the main road, by which time the pipe was going like a steam engine.

"Sharp, be damned," replied Rex. "That was the only way to deal. If I had started to haggle, we would have been there all day, especially when he knew we had the lorry with us. In any case, nobody down here would have bid him for the lot." I assumed, then, that they had been bought "half sensible".

Rex had been in an expansive mood going down but was even more so on the return journey. His pipe got so hot that on several occasions he had to hold it outside the window to cool down. We stopped just outside Exeter for a meal and, as we came down into Chideock, he suggested that we have a drink before going on home. We pulled up opposite the Bull Hotel in Bridport, crossed the road and entered the saloon bar. Rex ordered two whiskies and as he was being served he examined his pouch, which was virtually empty. "I'd better have a couple of ounces of St Julian, me dear; ain't got enough baccy to see me home" was his remark to the barmaid as she put out drinks on the bar. Two ounces in nine hours! As far as I know this was his record.

The shearlings did make a bob or two: we sold them at Ashford in October, at an average of one hundred and sixteen pounds each.

We did not go to Devon selling rams, as our main sales were Wilton, Findon and Kent, about sixty per cent being sold at Maidstone and Ashford. We always went to the Kent sales the previous day. I used to pick up Rex at Piddlehinton Cross at about ten o'clock in the morning, with the lorry already loaded. He would come up the road from Glebe House, stopping off at the village shop for his tobacco and half a pound of Fox's glacier mints, put his battered suitcase behind the seat in the cab and we were away. The journey was much slower then, for there was no M3, M25 or M20. We went via Salisbury, Winchester, the Hog's Back, Guildford, Redhill, Reigate, Westerham, Sevenoaks, Maidstone and Ashford. Rex "farmed" all the way there, and as we made the journey for four or five consecutive weeks he would comment on the progress of the arable work that was taking place.

One year he was seriously considering purchasing a chisel plough to use on the corn stubbles to help kill the couch and on several occasions we stopped when he spotted one being used alongside the road. Out he would get, have a look at the sort of job it was making, walk across, have a word with the tractor driver and pick his brains about the particular make of plough he was using.

As we continued our journey, he would pass his opinion: "Now that be a main useful tool, Shep. Better than the one we saw last week; got more clearance under the frame, won't bung up so easy as t'other did, and it's stronger. I'll have to find out how much they cost." The outcome was that he bought one for the next season and put it to work on the stubbles.

Jack Cox, a neighbouring farmer and contemporary of Rex, came to the farm in September to borrow a Southdown ram from me and while we were loading it up Rex arrived.

"See you got yourself a new toy" was Jack's greeting.

"That ain't no toy" came the rejoinder. "That be a main useful tool. We been through all the stubbles with it behind the combine and it ain't half cooked up the couch."

"What about the wild oats?" enquired Jack.

"What about 'em?" demanded Rex.

"Well, I'll tell 'ee," said Jack. "You gets on they stubbles before they oats have had time to germinate or the birds pick 'em up. Now that tool will put some of 'em down about an inch or two, they will come up next year; some will go down three or four inches for the year after; and some will go down six inches and they will be there for ever-lasting." He proved to be correct, for within three years, wild oats had become a major problem on that farm.

On one occasion, after selling at Maidstone, Mr Jim and Mr Bill Tory, Rex and I went to have a cup of tea before starting for home, leaving our three lorries parked side by side. When we returned we found, waiting by the lorries, a young man from the Customs and Excise, who requested permission to dip the lorry tanks to see that none contained red diesel. He dipped Mr Jim's and then Mr Bill's using a tiny little measure, about as big as a thimble, attached to a long, thin handle. He extracted a measure

164

from each lorry, examined it, found it to be in order and then tipped it away. He extracted the same tiny measure of diesel from our lorry, looked at it and was about to throw it away when Rex intervened: "Hold hard, young man. That do cost money. You put it back in the tank."

The trips back always followed the same pattern – a post mortem on the sale: whether it was good or bad, who had sold what and to whom, who had top price and who top average, the calculations being worked out on the back of a market card. We always stopped at a café on the Hog's Back for a cup of tea and a bun. After we left there, "farming" was restricted as the light was usually waning and the conversation turned to Rex's great love for fox hunting. He had followed the South Dorset Hunt since childhood and was, for many years, Chairman of the Hunt Committee. He knew every cover, earth, hunting gate and jump in the country and whenever the hounds were out between November and the end of February he would be there, right in front, regardless of the weather. To see him out hunting always reminded me of that great hunting print: "Handsome is as Handsome Does". There he'd be, slouching in the saddle, as though he were sitting in an armchair, with the bottom rein lying slack on his horse's neck. He would be dressed in a hunting jacket and cap that had started life as black, but which had been reduced to a dark green with the passage of time. His breeches were patched and his boots were a credit to the local harness maker, being more patches than boots! He rode a grand dark bay gelding called Sam – not the fastest galloper, but a great jumper with the heart of a lion: he would jump anything he was asked to. Together, they were a combination that kept up with any company.

I remember meeting Rex hacking back from hunting on a streaming wet January evening. It had been pouring with rain since about twelve o'clock and the land was completely waterlogged. Both horse and rider were covered in mud from head to foot and the water was running out of the tops of Rex's boots. He was absolutely soaked to the skin and even had his pipe turned upside down to keep out the rain. I ventured the suggestion that it had been a wet, miserable day. "I don't know about that, Shep. We had a wonderful day; never knowed better. I'll tell 'ee about it tomorrow. Can't stop now, won't do to let the horse get cold." And he ambled away into the gathering gloom, a very happy, if very wet, man.

After a day's hunting Rex would relate, in great detail, what had happened every inch of the way – where they had drawn, found, checked, gone to earth, lost the fox or killed. He would tell of the jumps he had taken (especially if the rest of the field had gone round them), the state of all the farms he had ridden over and the livestock he had seen.

Like most farmers, Rex liked to shoot, although it always took second place to his hunting. On one occasion he was shooting at Mr Jim Tory's farm when a fox came out of the kale and ran across in front of him. He raised his hat and wished it good morning. It went on through the hedge and in front of the next gun in the line, who was Mr Bill Tory. He too, raised his hat and wished him good day, then rolled him over, first barrel. Rex did not think too much of that!

On the evening before the annual Ram Show and Sale at Ashford, the auctioneers used to take the flock masters and shepherds who were selling next day out to dinner. At one of the events, Rex was sitting next to Bill Tory. During the course of the meal, Rex's tobacco pouch fell out of his back pocket and Mr Bill picked it up and pocketed it. After a while, Rex realised his loss and was hunting about under the table looking for it, ably assisted by Mr Bill, but without success. The next morning, as we went into the ring with our rams, John Martin, who was selling, announced from the box that the previous evening a tobacco pouch had been found and he was going to sell it, with the proceeds going to the Poppy Day Appeal. Rex promptly bid a pound and then the Tory brothers piled in and with a lot of good humour, banter and leg pulling, the bidding rose steadily to eight pounds, at which price Rex successfully purchased his own pouch!

That day we put fifteen rams through the ring to a really flying trade. As we got back to our pens, Rex emptied the remains of the tin of tobacco he had bought that morning into his pouch. He gazed at it for a moment, then a slow grin spread over his face. "They Tory boys thought they was smart, getting eight pounds out of I for my baccy pouch, but I reckon it put fifty pounds on they rams just now." Honour was restored.

We had ten bulling heifers to take back, which Rex had bought off Frank Tory. We made our usual stop on the Hog's Back for a cup of tea, then drove on to the Pheasant Inn, just to the east of Salisbury, where we always stopped for an evening meal. When we came out, Rex offered to drive the rest of the way, to which I readily agreed. On we went through Salisbury, down into Coombe Bissett, over Handley Cross and as we went down the hill into Cashmoor, the headlights picked up a dog fox as he meandered across the road. Rex slammed on the brakes, I nearly went through the windscreen and the heifers almost came through into the cab. The fox continued his stately progress across the road and up the bank, turned his head and appeared to give an appreciative nod, before disappearing into the hedge. Rex gravely lifted his hat and wished him good evening. I sat back in the seat rather shaken.

"What about they heifers?" I enquired.

"Oh, they'll be all right, none of 'em be in calf. This

gentleman will give someone a damn good run, one day. 'Tis a good job this lorry's got good brakes, though." The heifers were all right but whether or not the fox did give anyone a good run, no one knows.

Quite often on Sunday afternoons Rex, accompanied by his wife, would drive around the farm, arriving at the sheep when I was feeding up. The first spring we were together they came up on Palm Sunday. It was a beautiful April day and we had a grand lot of lambs still with their mothers, just finishing off the swedes. The lambs had just had their corn and were lined up on the troughs like soldiers on parade; the ewes in the back fold were similarly standing to the hay racks chewing away. We stood looking at them for several minutes in silence. Rex removed his pipe from his mouth. "Now that's what I call a pretty picture, Shep. By God, that's a smart bunch of lambs." He took a few puffs on his pipe, savouring the picture before him. "Them lambs we sent off on Tuesday weighed well." (That week we had sold quite a number of fat lambs that were not required for flock replacements or were not up to standard for rams and they had realised an exceptionally high price.)

We continued to stand, looking at the peaceful scene before us, then Mrs Lovelace remarked that during all their married life they had never had one of their own lambs for Easter. I assured her that if she wanted one it could be found.

Rex interrupted: "There ain't none left that's fit. We sold 'em all this week that were good enough."

"Yes, there is," I replied. "I ain't going to keep that thick dark-headed ewe lamb; she's blacker than old Stewart's Hamps."

Rex grunted and tried a new tack: "If you have one, my dear, we shall have to take it to Dorchester to get it killed and dressed, then fetch it back and get someone to cut it

168

up. It ain't worth all the hassle."

"There's no need to take one to Dorchester. I can dress it here and cut it up if you wish," I replied. After a bit more persuasion, Rex reluctantly agreed.

The lamb was duly killed and dressed on Wednesday and on Good Friday I cut it up and received a shoulder for my trouble. On Sunday afternoon they were round again. Mrs Lovelace enquired if we'd had our shoulder of lamb for lunch and I assured her that we had and that it had been excellent.

"So was ours," she replied, then turning to Rex: "Wasn't it dear?"

"Yes" he replied, then, taking another pull at his pipe, added as an afterthought: "But 'twer like eating money."

A Man's Best Friend

FOR the last forty years the same family of Scottish Border Collies have been my constant faithful companions – we now have the sixth generation working. In all that time we have only gone completely outside on one occasion, line breeding the dogs the same as we do the sheep. One of the great attractions of this line is their temperament; we have not had a bad-tempered one yet. For me, life without two or three collies about would be unthinkable and unbearable.

As I write, four bitches are lying asleep on the rugs around the fire and Bob is sprawled out on the settee. I have never subscribed to the theory that it spoils working dogs if they are allowed in the house and treated as pets. After a hard day's work I appreciate a little comfort and I am sure that they do too – and when they get past work, we always retire them and they become house dogs in their old age, staying at home with Dorothy, toddling over the road to see the sheep or up to the village shop or post office. As a rule we seem to have two old pensioners about and when the younger generation returns from work they adopt a very superior and condescending air towards them. Like all animals and humans they are individuals, each with their different ways and temperament. Dorothy always feeds them and looks after the puppies – we generally have a litter most years.

Again, contrary to a lot of professional opinion, I start to break pups to work at about five months old, taking them out with a good, older dog. But even by that age Dorothy will have schooled them in basic manners. In other words, they know their name, will come when called, sit when told, stop on command and walk to heel without a lead.

When we were living in Dorchester I had a grand four-year-old bitch named Bess, which Dorothy always made a great fuss of. For several weeks I worked away from home, going on Monday morning and returning Friday evening. The first week I took Bess up with me, she worked perfectly all day but refused to eat her meal that evening when we failed to take her home. The next day she flatly refused to work at all. This went on all week, with Bess eating virtually nothing and showing no intention of doing any work. As soon as we returned on Friday evening, her appetite returned to normal. She never would work properly for me again, but for Dorothy she would do anything. She made it very obvious that she had no intention of leaving home again and spent ten years of her life as my wife's constant companion and guardian.

In all the years we have kept collies there have only been three dogs, Bob, Bruce and Bob again. They have all been extremely good but the best was undoubtedly Old Bob who was, I suppose, the founder of the dynasty. We had him as an eight-week-old pup and set about training him in the usual way; he was almost six months old when I started to take him out to work. For the next six months he nearly drove me mad. He was quite obedient and did exactly as he was told, but showed no interest whatever in either sheep or cattle. I was beginning to wonder if he would ever work. Then one day, after dinner, I went to see the ewes who were running along a narrow field at the bottom of the farm, taking Bob with me. We opened the gate, went in and then, more in hope than anything else, I told him to come by and to my amazement off he went, following the hedge round until he was behind the ewes and bringing them right up to the gate. I could not believe my eyes. I called him to heel and made a great fuss of him, then took him right down to the bottom of the field and sent him away for a second time. Again he gathered perfectly and brought the flock back down the field to me – and from that day on he never put a foot wrong.

At Newburgh, when we drove the sale rams down to the building for their final trim, this often entailed a walk of up to a mile. One morning we had just got out on to the farm road with a dozen rams when Billy Boss arrived unexpectedly with a customer who wanted a ram. Thinking that the deal would not take long, we left the rams with Bob on the track and returned to the fold. The sale took longer than expected, because the old boy could not make up his mind which one to have. However, he decided eventually, we loaded it into his Land Rover and I shot off in the van to find out where Bob and the rams were. I got out onto the track; no Bob, no rams and none anywhere in sight. Looking around, it was obvious that they had gone downhill by the droppings, so off I went. The dairyman was coming out of a field just above the building where he had been moving on his electric fence.

"Here, Dennis, have you seen that fool dog of mine with a bunch of rams?" I asked.

"They went past here half an hour ago. He took 'em round back of the barn" came the reply.

Round the back of the cottages I went, into the yard behind the barn, on one side of which was situated the trimming shed, and there in the shed, all lying down, were the rams with Bob sitting in the doorway. He had brought those rams down the track for a good mile, past numerous open gateways and three side roads, around the cottages, into the yard and put them into the shed, all on his own.

We never again walked rams to the shed ourselves. When we needed them at the building, we used to put them out on the road with Bob, go back to the sheep house for breakfast and after breakfast drive down to the trimming shed, always to find the sheep penned and Bob on guard. The old boy was a great, strong dog with a wonderful temperament, but he would stand no nonsense from either man or beast.

Foreman Hanger had a wire-haired terrier which, like most terriers, was all yap and no sense. The little fool was always picking fights with Bob, who used to lift him up and shake him like a rat. He always came back for more, though. We were trimming one afternoon and Bob was stretched out asleep in the sun, without a care in the world, when who should come into the yard but Foreman Hanger with his dog. The silly ass made straight for Bob and started a fight and, as usual, was getting a hiding, when the foreman intervened, giving Bob a good belt in the ribs with his walking stick. Now this was asking for trouble, as it is an unwritten law that only a shepherd is allowed to correct his own dog. But before I could say or do anything, Bob took the matter in hand himself. He dropped the terrier, spun round and, as the foreman lifted his stick to take another swipe, he leapt, catching the stick in his jaws in mid-air and wrenching it from the man's hand. He landed, spat it out and then, with his lips turned up, every tooth showing and every hair from his neck to his tail standing up straight, he advanced slowly, backing the petrified foreman up against the barn wall. Never before in my life have I seen such contained hatred in an animal. I was fearful of what would happen next and shouted "Sit." He sat instantly, but without taking his eyes off the foreman, or uttering a sound. "Heel," I called. He obediently came to heel and rubbed his head into my leg as if to say: "Sorry about that, but I'm not taking that treatment from anyone." The foreman was shaking like a leaf, but I was so relieved that I did not tell him off; but

173

Arthur gave him a right rollicking.

When we moved to Piddlehinton, Bob was getting on and semi-retired but still a great road dog, especially with cattle. Several times I had helped Rex move young stock, until one day he wanted assistance when I was extra busy, so I suggested that he took Bob – the old boy would work for anyone. Off they went in the Land Rover, Robert sitting up in the passenger seat, monarch of all he surveyed. This was the start of a great partnership. Whenever cattle had to be moved, off they would go, Bob rounding them up and driving them out onto the road. Rex would then drive slowly in front, the cattle coming on behind and Bob bringing up the rear and then, to his great satisfaction, he would spend the rest of the day riding around in the Land Rover.

As he got older, his sight began to fail. By then he was completely retired, with the exception of one little job he always did. Two cows were kept in a small paddock adjoining the cottage. I used to milk out what we wanted for ourselves and then put calves on them. Bob's job was to fetch them in, but after a while he got them properly trained. While I was putting their corn in the manger he would slip out under the gate, trot about fifty yards out into the field and bark. Up would go their heads and on they would come, with the old boy toddling behind.

When we were at Newburgh, one little bitch almost got me into trouble with the law. I was going back from lunch and had to stop at the local ironmonger to get a tin of paint which we required for marking sale sheep. In those days, I had a Morris 1000 van and Fly always used to curl up right behind the driving seat. I had left the van pulled in outside the shop and on coming out found our local policeman standing beside it. The thought flashed through my mind that he must have found something wrong with the van. I don't know why, but I always get a guilty conscience whenever I find a policeman looking at my vehicle.

I wished him good afternoon and he proceeded to tear me off a strip. "Just look here," he said, "not only did you leave this van unattended and unlocked, but you also left your keys in the ignition. Anyone could have driven it away; it is just asking for it to be stolen. I suggest that in future you show more responsibility."

"But, Officer," I protested, "no one can drive that van away."

"Don't be stupid," he snapped. "All they have to do is open the door, turn the key and drive off."

"You try, then," I suggested, all innocent-like.

The policeman opened the door with his right hand, put his left on the steering wheel and started to get into the seat, when suddenly and without a sound, a black head with a white blaze shot up over the back of the seat and with a flash of white teeth and a sharp smack, a pair of jaws snapped shut about two inches in front of his face. He retreated out of that van like a scalded cat. Somewhat shaken he grumbled: "You did not tell me you had a dog in there."

"You didn't bloody well ask" was the reply he got. After that little run-in, we got on quite well.

When the boys were growing up, the dogs contributed to our income. I always had two working dogs that were never for sale, but also a couple of youngsters coming on which, when working, were sold. There was then, and still is, always someone wanting a broken dog; so many people never think about a replacement until something happens to the one they have and then they suddenly realise how true is the old saying: "You never know how good a dog is until you have lost him." Back in those days, you could get twenty pounds for a decent working young dog. That may not sound much today, but then it represented two weeks' wages.

In the late fifties I was at Exeter market one Friday ram selling, when a local farmer had two smart collie pups for sale – not our type of collie but the short-coated, tricolour Devon sort. Harold, a friend who was also ram selling and was looking for a pup, was interested in them. We had a good look at them and they seemed perfectly all right, but there had to be a catch somewhere, for they were not being sold at the usual eight to ten weeks' old, but were all of six months. The auctioneer tried to sell them, putting them up at a pound and running them on up to twenty-nine shillings. At that stage, Harold was going to bid. "Here, hang on," I cautioned. "He ain't got that, he's been taking them bids off the wall." Sure enough, he had not got a bid and had to withdraw them. Harold still wanted one, in spite of the fact that they should have made a lot more money and no one local had bid for them. "Let's go and rub that in to him," I suggested. So we descended on the owner and suggested that there had to be something wrong somewhere. After a bit I enquired what was the lowest he would take. He said that he had been bid twenty-nine shillings, but the least he would take was thirty. "Come off it, we were not born yesterday," I replied. "Old Fred never had a bid, he was talking to himself. Tell 'ee what, I'll give 'ee thirty bob for the pair." And, much to my surprise, he accepted. There had to be a catch in it somewhere, but at fifteen shillings each it was worth a gamble.

Catch there was, sure enough, which we both found out as soon as we got them home. The blasted things would catch and kill chickens for fun. Mine had three in the first two days. I gave him a good hiding each time with the dead chicken, with no effect whatever. If he caught sight of a chicken he was after it. The governor suggested that the only way to stop him was to shoot him and I was beginning to think that he was right. But the suggestion of shooting him put an idea into my head. I opened up a cartridge, shook out all the lead shot and replaced it with half a dozen dried peas that we were cracking for the lambs. Then I let the dog out into the orchard at the back of our cottage where Dorothy had her Aylesbury ducks. Off he went and started to beat hell out of them. I waited a second or two, until he had his tail towards me, and then let him have it right up his backside. Over he went, then up he got "pie pie-ing", straight through the orchard hedge into the road, up the sunken lane to the church, back down the hill into the village, down the main street and home into his kennel, making the round trip of nearly a mile in a couple of minutes. He had a sore backside for days, but never again chased either ducks or chickens. Within six months he was working well and we sold him.

The only time that the dogs have let me down was a few years ago when I was shearing with George Payne and Mark Olaf. We had finished one flock and moved onto another on the same farm. When we arrived, the sheep had not been penned and were still out in a nearby field. It was one of those family farms with all Chiefs and no Indians, so out I went with two bitches and a pup to gather up the ewes and lambs. The damn things would not move anyhow, much to the delight of George and Mark. According to them, the pup chased a rabbit, one scratched her backside and the other went to sleep, but they decided to give me one out of ten for trying. It was not really as bad as that, but those ewes would stand to a dog for fun.

I suppose I must be getting soft in my old age, for now I cannot bring myself to sell a dog once I have broken it in, for by then they have become part of the family. We still have a litter of pups most years, and I am quite happy to see them go, but an older dog is a different story. We have always had a Nellie – four of them in all. The last one passed away a couple of months ago. But at this moment we have a litter of pups and in spite of my insistence that none of them are to be kept, I hear Dorothy calling one Little Nellie. I have a terrible feeling that we shall not be without a Nellie for much longer . . .

And since writing this I have to say that we *do* have a Nellie, now two years old and a grand working bitch!

The College

FOR my sins, for several years I was shepherd at an Agricultural College. Looking back, it was a mistake on my part and I should have known better than to think that I would fit into the system. I tried to kid myself that I would be able to pass on some of my practical experience to students but, really, the position had two greater attractions, one being that it was pensionable (I was fifty and beginning to think about the time when I should have to retire). Also a really good, modern cottage went with the job.

The flock consisted of three hundred Dorset Horn ewes, lambing in October. About one hundred and twenty chilver lambs and a dozen ram lambs were retained annually and the ram lambs were sold at the Society's May Fair. The rest of the lamb crop was disposed of as spring lambs, with as many as possible catching the Easter market, when the price was at its peak.

The flock was used as a break in the arable rotation. Each year some forty acres of one-year ley were under-sown in the corn. Twenty acres of rye were grown, followed by kale and swedes, plus twenty acres of stubble turnips behind winter barley. As the ewes lambed in early October, they were moved onto the maiden seeds, over which they were folded. By the end of November they went into the stubble turnips, which lasted to mid-January, when they were again moved into the kale and swedes. These were finished by mid-March, by which time all the

179

fat lambs had been sold. The ewes and replacement chilver lambs then fed off the rye for a month before going back onto the maiden seeds for the summer. The swede and stubble turnip ground was sown with spring barley and the rye ground was prepared for the planting of swedes and kale for the next winter.

The flock was folded throughout the year, using wire netting on the roots and rye and, during the summer only, electrified wire on the grass. The reason for this is that the electrified wire is held up by plastic stakes with quarter-inch diameter metal ends about four inches long, which are pushed into the ground. In the less consolidated root ground it was a job to get them to hold firmly enough to keep the wire upright and a path had to be pulled or cut through the roots to stop the wire shorting out. If this happened the ewes seemed to sense that there was no current running through the wire and they were soon out. During the summer, when folding grass, the stakes held much better in the firm ground and I used to cut paths for the wire through the grass with a mowing machine behind a tractor, generally cutting enough paths to last a week at a time. After the grass in these paths had been cut a day or two and wilted, it was the first thing the sheep would eat every morning when let on to the next fold.

It was a very simple system that made the most use of the land, giving a valuable break in the arable rotation and increasing the fertility of the soil, but its greatest drawback was that it was labour intensive. In fact, it took nearly as much labour as a comparable-sized Down flock, which would have been producing up to one hundred ram lambs for sale, with a subsequently larger income.

Most of the ewes lambed outside on grass. If the weather broke towards the end of October the few that were left were moved into a barn at night. Each day, a line of hurdle square pens were pitched up inside the fold, into which the ewes were put with their lambs as they were born. The next day – by which time the lambs had sucked and mothered up – they were turned out in front and after a few more days were turned away into the new seeds. The hours of daylight were almost the same as during the March lambing, but it was always much warmer than in the spring and most of the lambs were born before the middle of the month. They were some two months old by the time they went into the stubble turnips. These were always direct-drilled into a winter barley stubble so there was much less mud than would be experienced in roots, for which the land had been freshly ploughed. By the time they went into roots proper in mid-January, many of the lambs were almost fit to sell and quite big and strong enough to stand the mud.

As they lambed, the ewes were split up. Those with twins were put in one fold, those with single wether lambs in another, about a dozen of the best male lambs were retained for rams and kept separate, and the ewes with single ewe lambs were joined up with the hoggets in another fold. This enabled both the ewes and their lambs to be fed according to their requirements; the ram lambs were pushed hardest and the single ewe lambs least.

The farm manager was a great arable farmer and we always had good crops of roots but, from a shepherd's point of view, he had one great failing: he could not make good hay to save his life, putting all his faith in machinery and not enough in the weather. The same day as the grass was cut he was in with a hay bob, tedding the grass out of swathe, kicking it from here to breakfast time, repeating the exercise several times a day. I grant you he got it fit to bale a day or two sooner than the conventional way, but all that was left was a lot of bruised and squashed stalks with all the leaf beaten off. What a difference from the clover hay at Newburgh and Piddlehinton.

It was a grand flock of ewes, there was plenty of grub and it was the best farm to grow sheep on that I have ever worked. The system was comparatively easy to operate, we had a good house and made a decent wage. I should have been satisfied, but somehow it was not my cup of tea. I had worked for three of the best flock masters in the south-west and been used to meeting them before breakfast every day, when any problems were sorted out to our mutual satisfaction. If any major decisions had to be made they were made then and there, with an answer straight away. In other words, you went straight to the engine driver. At a college, however, it was rather like farming by committee. Things tended to go round and round and with a bit of luck either got lost, or by the time an answer was received it would be too late for it to be implemented. An old friend of mine has the right idea about committees. He maintains that a committee should consist of an uneven number of people and that three is too many. This was, I think, the thing that made me feel so unsettled and insecure. I believe that nothing can replace the personal relationship that exists between an employer and employee who have mutual trust and respect for each other; when you work for a county council you tend to become a number on a card and no longer a person.

There were between thirty and forty full-time students in residence. Each week, a group of four came out with the sheep for an hour before breakfast and three hours in the afternoon. Each group spent one week every term with the flock. You were lucky if you had ten or a dozen that were really interested in sheep; the others tended to be a captive audience. This was to be expected, as most students were the sons and daughters of local farmers and farmworkers and we were in an area where the dairy cow reigned supreme – and sheep were still at that time the Cinderella of the livestock industry. It was only natural that most students took most interest in the enterprise they had at home.

For the last ten years, I have done quite a lot of practical sheep instruction and lecturing for the Agricultural Training Board and it is something that I have come to quite enjoy doing. I find that there are three great differences between this and college work: the students are older and therefore more mature; they come because they want to learn; and finally, and perhaps most important, they have had to pay to attend. Besides enjoying this, I appear to have become quite popular – in any case they keep on asking me to come back again, whereas I am afraid I was not the most popular member of the farm staff at college.

Looking back, some of the blame must be mine in that I was, and hope still am, a bit of a perfectionist. It was impossible to work for men like Bill Hooper and Rex Lovelace and not be. On the other hand, I would not grumble at how long it took the students to do a job, but I did expect it to be done properly. I would never ask anyone to do something that I was not prepared and able to do myself. There was one other point that I insisted on which did not endear me to the students. After being addressed respectfully by my employers for the last twenty years as Shepherd or Shep, I was damned certain that no student was going to call me by my Christian name. The only other instruction that I had given at that time was to my son David and I like to think that I made a fair job of that, as he has turned out, in my opinion, a better sheep man than me. Admittedly he spent two years at Agricultural Colleges, although I have always maintained that amongst other things, he learned to drink beer and smoke cigarettes at one and to drink whisky and smoke a pipe at the other! Needless to say, the second college was in the north.

Then two things happened that changed my entire life.

At the time I thought they meant the end of the world for me and for a time left me very bitter and demoralised, but they turned out very much for the best and allowed me to realise a life-long dream. I believe they demonstrated the truth of that old saying "Every cloud has a silver lining." First I had an accident at work with a transport box on the back of a tractor, injuring my back. I was on and off work for over a year. The doctors prescribed rest, pain-killing drugs, put me in a corset and manipulated my back under anaesthetic, all to no avail; a few weeks back at work and I would be in agony again. At the same time, we lost two ewes with scrapie and the governors in their wisdom decided that the entire flock had to be slaughtered. To have a flock that you have bred, worked and worried over destroyed in this manner is heartbreaking, especially when you personally have doubts as to the necessity of such drastic action. I often wonder if the governors and their advisers would have pursued the same course of action if it had been their own flock. At the time, it left me very disillusioned and I still consider it was the unnecessary destruction of a grand flock of sheep.

With the flock gone and no plans for its replacement I was made redundant and, as we lived in a tied cottage, we had to move out of our home. We were, however, very lucky to be offered a house on a temporary basis until we could obtain something permanent; this was a time when houses were in short supply and if one came on the market it was sold in a matter of days.

Rock Bottom and Climbing Out

WHEN I was made redundant, my world fell to pieces. I was without a job, my back was stopping me from taking another similar post and I had no qualifications or experience in any other occupation. Worst of all, we had no permanent home. Life looked rather bleak and I wondered whatever I had done to deserve the mess we found ourselves in. This, I believe, is the worst aspect of the tied cottage; if, through no fault of your own, you are unable to continue with your employment not only are you out of a job, but also without a home.

This was the first time in my life that things started to get on top of me and I began to indulge in self-pity. Luckily, however, I was brought back to my senses by a chance remark. An old friend, after enquiring how my back was, suggested that I would have to get something lighter to do and thought that I could obtain a position as a petrol pump attendant. This gave me quite a jolt. Here was I at fifty-five and they thought I was on the scrap heap and were writing me off. Well, if I could not manage a hurdled flock any more there must be other things within the sheep industry that I could do. After thirty years of shepherding I was damned if I was going to finish up on a garage forecourt selling petrol; I was reminded of my mother's words: "'Tis better to live in spite than in pity."

The first thing that I did after being made redundant was to help a local farmer, Tom Merchant, lamb some five hundred Welsh cross ewes. Lambing took place out of doors, similar to the Kent set-up, the only difference being that in the evening the in-lamb ewes were brought into a small paddock adjoining the farmhouse where they could be kept under observation during the night. I was getting about with some difficulty and was in considerable pain. On the second day, Tom suggested that I should go and see a physiotherapist who had treated him with success. I had been very dubious about going to anyone except a doctor, taking the view that if they could not put me right, who could? But Tom would not take no for an answer and made an appointment for me that evening. The visit was a turning point. For two years my back had given me hell; I had taken enough pain-killing tablets to sink a battleship but as soon as I put any strain on it I was doubled up. I am convinced that, but for this treatment, I should not have been able to continue work in the way I have done. I used to go back for treatment every few months, but as time went on these visits became less frequent and for the last two years I have not had to return.

Shortly after my back began to improve, we managed to buy a small terraced house on the outskirts of Dorchester. It was not what we really wanted, but at least it was a home of our own, although living in a town after spending over fifty years in the country was quite a change – and a change that I did not enjoy. What I could not get used to was the lack of space. Dorothy always tells me that I am very untidy and leave things lying about and, as usual, she is right. After farm buildings and a large garden, to suddenly find yourself in a house that opens onto a busy pavement, with only a pocket-sized garden at the back and no back kitchen in which to kick off your muddy boots and wet coats when you come home, takes a lot of getting used to. It did, though, remove the greatest worry that I had ever had, that of being without a roof over our heads.

While at the college, I had instigated a course on the preparation of sheep for show and sale. The courses were held during the holidays, when there were no students in residence, and they had proved very popular and successful, being over-subscribed on both occasions. It was at the time when a lot of people were coming into pedigree sheep in a small way and doing their own shepherding, but very few, if any, had any experience in turning out sheep for show or sale, especially rams.

Shortly after leaving the college, I was approached by the Agricultural Training Board, which suggested that I became one of their instructors, with the emphasis on pedigree sheep. I agreed with some trepidation and was sent on a residential course, not to learn anything about sheep, but to get a grounding in passing on knowledge – teacher training, I suppose they call it. It was like going back to school again.

There were about a dozen of us and I was the odd one out in as much as I was old enough to be everyone else's father but, to my amazement, I thoroughly enjoyed myself. We were worked fairly hard and had quite a bit of written work to do in the evenings. The hotel accommodation was quite good and after dinner on the first evening we all adjourned to the bar. After a couple of drinks everyone, with the exception of the instructors, excused themselves to finish their written work. I stayed on, took the pants off the instructors at the card game nap and drank them under the table, woke up early next morning, finished the written work and went down to breakfast as fresh as a daisy. The instructors came down looking much the worse for wear. Someone commented on their appearance at breakfast and received a warning: "Don't ever play cards or drink with grandad; he has got X-ray eyes and a gut made of cast iron." I took it as quite a compliment.

Since that time, I have continued to do quite a lot of instruction with pedigree sheep in all parts of the country and it is very rewarding when I see former pupils bringing out their sheep in a proper manner.

I also got involved in preparing sheep for the Wool Board TV commercials, making several trips to film studios and on one never-to-be-forgotten occasion, spending four days in Snowdonia, filming on location. The first time that I went into a film studio it was quite an eye-opener, to see how the industry worked. A film was being made depicting the four seasons, using different types and weights of cloth for spring, summer, autumn and winter. It was my job to prepare a sheep as it would look for the different seasons. For winter we had her in full fleece, then about one-third of her wool was trimmed off for autumn, about half of what was left came off for summer and she was clean-shorn for spring. This all sounds easy, but I can assure you that to cut off a third of a sheep's wool evenly all over without leaving any blow marks is quite an art and is very time consuming. The conditions I worked under were wonderful; I was waited on constantly, with electricians to move the lights around, tea and coffee available at all times and meals in the canteen that would not have disgraced a three-star hotel.

As for the actual filming, there seemed to be a never-ending number of technicians, about sixteen in all. It looked to me, as a simple countryman, that about four did the work and the rest gave orders and argued amongst themselves. In another commercial, we had to get a ram to run up what looked like a steep hill to a ewe on the top. The hill had been constructed in the studio from scaffolding covered with planks which had turf laid on them and it looked very realistic; the ramp was some twenty yards long with a gradient of one in five. The ewe and ram had been kept apart right up to the time of

188

shooting, then the ewe was placed on top of the artificial hill and tethered with a short length of fishing line around one foot. The ram was supposed to run up the hill to join her. Before we started, it was pointed out to the director that he had to get it right first time because there was little chance of a re-run. Anyway, off we went, with the old ewe "baa-ing" away on her own at the top of the hill. The ram, sensing a "bit of the other", curled back his lips and charged up the hill without any hesitation. Arriving at the top he had a sniff and lost all interest in the ewe. The director seemed pleased but asked for a re-take, and in spite of my assurance that the ram would not do it again, insisted that we try. The ram was brought down, the cameras rolled, but he had no intention of running up the hill again for nothing. The director wanted to know why. I replied: "If you had climbed up a drainpipe to spend a night with your girlfriend and had the window slammed in your face would you turn around and climb up again?" I don't think that a countryman's uncouth humour was appreciated.

The most enjoyable time that we spent filming was four wonderful days on location in Snowdonia, right out on the open mountainside. The first day was foggy, but then the weather cleared and we had three beautiful, sunny days. We had brought a sheep up with us and for the film he had to stand on different parts of the hill, either on rock outcrops or high vantage points. The only way that he could be tethered was tying him by his foot with a fine piece of line, which under no circumstance had to be visible on the film. I was worried that he would become frightened and break the line, or pull up the little peg to which the line was attached and make off across the open mountain. I had not brought a dog with me, and if the ram *had* got loose I am sure that we should still be up there looking for him.

One year, while I was still at the college, I met Harry Ransom at the Dorchester May Fair, where I was selling rams. I had known him by sight for some years as head horseman for Young's Brewery. He introduced himself and asked if I could help him. I enquired in what way. "I am looking for a pretty ram," he replied. My immediate reaction was "We've got a right one here," but he went on to explain that Young's Ram Brewery at Wandsworth had as their mascot a Horn Ram. The old one had died and he had been sent down to purchase a replacement. The two most important yardsticks were that he had to be pretty and very docile. I had a ram in my pen that was a trifle short but otherwise fitted the bill very well; and to cut a long story short, Harry bought him. This started a relationship with Harry and Young's Brewery that has continued to this day.

In February 1981, to celebrate the one hundred and fiftieth anniversary of the foundation of the brewery, the Queen paid a visit, toured the establishment and inspected the heavy horse stable. On the previous Thursday I'd gone to London and trimmed the ram especially for the occasion. At lunch-time on Sunday the 'phone rang and a very agitated Harry was on the other end: "This ram is blown up like a barrel and frothing at the mouth. He's got something stuck in his throat and I can't move it." I suggested that he cut off about two feet of his garden hose and try gently to push the obstruction down. Twenty minutes later the 'phone went again. Harry was back. The ram had died before he had returned with the hose.

"That's going to be awkward for you. The Queen's coming on Wednesday and you haven't got a mascot," I ventured.

"Not as awkward as it is for you" came the rejoinder. "I've been on to the governor and his instructions are that he wants a replacement here by Tuesday. It has to be pretty, quiet and turned out properly, so pull your finger out and get on with it." This was at one o'clock on a streaming wet Sunday in February.

Within an hour I had located and bought a suitable ram, but he was outside in roots, wet through and covered in mud. Sunday afternoon was spent washing him, for he was in the devil of a mess. Then he had to be dried, so we put him in a well-bedded loose box overnight. Monday morning came and it was still raining, so there was no chance of turning him outside in the wind to dry off. We tied him up under two infra-red lamps, almost cooking him, but by evening he was dry enough to be cut to shape. I left home with him early next morning and arrived at Wandsworth before eight, and by early afternoon I had him looking a treat. The governor was delighted and invited Dorothy and me to come up on the Wednesday, when I had the honour of being presented to Her Majesty.

During the period immediately after leaving the college I returned for a time to my old love, horses, looking after a small stud of Shires, consisting of a couple of brood mares and several youngsters. We also worked a stallion, in a season covering some thirty mares. We had a very successful season, winning an impressive array of rosettes and several cups. I had not put up a horse's mane or tail since the early fifties, some twenty-odd years before, but it is surprising how quickly the old skills return.

On arriving at a show, the horses were unloaded and tied to the side of the lorry, to which metal feed bins were clipped, a feed put in and a start made to washing out their legs, using soap powder and warm water. All the hair, or feather as it is called, was made spotless, then white sawdust was rubbed in to facilitate drying. While the legs were drying out a start was made in putting up the manes. For this, a long bunch of raffia was used, replacing the wheat straw of my youth. Standing on a stool alongside the horse's withers, one took three single strands of raffia and, with a few hairs from the forelock, plaited up two fine cords of hair and raffia. Then the bunch of long raffia was laid down the neck and tied tightly at the top with the two plaited cords. The bunch was next divided into three equal skeins for plaiting. Every time the top skein was brought down to the middle, as this was being done, a few hairs from the mane were twisted in with it and every time a flyer was inserted into the plait. These flyers consisted of a double bow of ribbon mounted on a short wire. When this was finished, there was a plait of raffia firmly held by the hair of the mane, lying on the crest of the neck from forelock to withers, with about ten flyers standing up about two inches above the raffia.

Putting up tails was vastly different from what it had been twenty years before, when most heavy horses had their tails docked. This practice is now illegal. With the long tail, the practice is to clip the bottom half of the tail hair right off and plait up what is left to form a bun at the top, then tie it off with ribbons. Once the mane and tail were up, the sawdust was brushed out of the legs and the horse given a brush down with a dandy brush, and a final wipe with a cloth dampened with paraffin. He was then ready to be judged.

The horses were led clockwise around the ring with the judge standing in the middle. After he had watched them closely for a time, he drew them out in order of preference, lining them up across the ring. They were then handled for faults or blemishes, particular attention being paid to their hooves and legs. Next they were individually walked up and down and then trotted up and down, placed in their final order and the rosettes given out, after which the winner led off out. This is known as "judging in hand".

We also used to participate in the harness class. This is

for a horse in breeching harness and, believe me, there is a huge amount of work involved both at home and on the show field, in keeping a set of show harnesses up to scratch. All the leather has to be cleaned and polished inside and out, then the harness brasses on the blind halter, breeching, chest strap, loin strap, apron and leading reins have to be polished. Finally the steel tug chains, breeching chains and back chain are burnished. It takes a whole day to do it properly.

The procedure of harnessing up went something like this. First the collar was slipped over the horse's head and twisted the right way up so that it fitted snugly on the back of the shoulder. When in place, there had to be enough room at the bottom for a person's arm to slide in between the collar and the horse's neck. The brass hames were fixed onto the collar by means of a chain and hook at the bottom and a leather pole strap at the top. Then came the breeching harness – first a cart saddle across the back, just behind the withers, kept in position by a leather belly band around the horse's ribs. From the cart saddle a wide strap ran down the back almost to the tail and from this four narrow straps, two each side, went down over the loins to join another wide strap that went around the back end of the horse. These straps were joined by breeching chains to the shafts of a cart so that, when going downhill, the horse could hold back a load by sitting back in the breeching. The actual working harness was completed by the blind halter which was, in effect, a bridle with leather blinkers attached that stopped the horse from seeing behind and to the side.

Then came the decorations: a wide breast strap from the bottom of the collar to the belly band with up to half a dozen brasses attached and a brass buckle each end; a leather apron behind the top of the hames covered in small brasses; bells on the top of the blind halter; a loin strap behind the cart saddle, again containing half a dozen brasses; a pair of leading reins from the bit in the blind halter to the D-ring in the end of the back strap; and a pair of driving reins coiled onto the hames. The harness itself had ten brass buckles and over twenty brasses.

The Valley of the Bride

WE had settled down in our little terraced house in Dorchester and I was finding enough work to pay our way, but I was far from happy. I managed to keep in touch and was still involved in the pedigree sheep world, but I was not able to participate. It is a rotten feeling when you have been at the top of your profession for a number of years suddenly to find that you have become a has-been, and I resented it very much. Our younger son, Russell, who had married a couple of years previously, was also living in Dorchester, in a house very similar to our own. They had just had their first child, our first grandson, and were also looking for a home in the country.

Russell heard of a large farmhouse that was up for sale in the village where he was working and after protracted negotiations we managed to purchase it.

In April 1982 we moved to Charity Farm House, Litton Cheney, the same house where my uncle had been born some ninety years before. Litton Cheney is a picture-postcard village of old stone houses with little streams running alongside the village streets. Situated some ten miles west of Dorchester, it nestles in the centre of the valley of the Bride, a beautiful area of water meadows, little streams, small hedged fields and grazing cattle stretching from the source of the Bride of Little Bredy, until it enters the sea at Burton Bradstock. The river, as it meanders through the valley, is joined by no less than nine little tributaries in its six-mile length. The valley, never more then two miles wide, is bounded on the south by the coastal ridge and on the north by the high chalk hills over which the main Dorchester to Bridport road runs and under which the village shelters. It is a bit of a backwater, being virtually untouched by the modern holiday traffic which races along the A35, a mile to the north, on its way to Devon and Cornwall, or moves up the coast road a mile to the south. No one of any consequence or importance has ever been born or lived here, so by and large we are spared the inconvenience of sightseers and day trippers.

Charity Farm House, reputed to be the oldest house in the village, stands a few yards back from the road which has a stream running down the opposite side. Dating from the early 1600s, it is a long, narrow, Dorset farmhouse, with two-foot thick stone walls, cut stone quoins and lintels, roofed with stone tiles and slate, with long oak beams spanning its width from front to back. These beams all have Roman numerals cut into them and holes and mortices that bear no relationship to their present use or position. These beams, the large quoins and the lintels lead me to believe that the house is a classic example of seventeenth-century recycling.

We converted this lovely old building into two homes; Russell, his wife and three sons live in one, Dorothy and I in the other. The conversion took five years to complete, with Russell doing most of the work himself, besides having a full-time job. He was responsible for most of the planning and design of the alterations, ably assisted by his mother, who has always considered that architects have no idea how the interior of a house should be designed. The attraction of the living room in both houses has been greatly enhanced by the inglenook fireplaces that we found, which had been boarded up. Now opened up again, and with the oak beams exposed, they have added great character to these rooms.

When we first moved in everything was very basic, including the plumbing. On our first night, I awoke in the early hours of the morning to the sound of running water. Thinking that the pipes had sprung a leak and with visions of water everywhere, I jumped out of bed in a devil of a tear, waking Dorothy, who enquired what the panic was all about. "Can't you hear that water running?" I replied. "A pipe must have broken somewhere."

She listened for a second, rolled over and proceeded to go back to sleep, quietly muttering: "It's the stream, you bloody old fool!"

Shortly after moving to Litton, I had the opportunity to rent eight acres of land, with a building, adjoining our house. It was an offer that I could not refuse and a small flock of pedigree Dorset Down ewes was purchased. David had had the Southdowns for several years by now and I could not see the sense in going into competition with him. In any case, he might have beaten me and that would never do! Another point in favour of the Dorset Downs was that they were relatively inexpensive to buy. This was the second time that I had endeavoured to start a pedigree flock and I am afraid that circumstances dictated that I took a completely different approach. Instead of buying just a few really good ewes, I bought twenty-four cheap ones, but from two extremely good breeders. I went down to the Devon border to purchase fourteen full mouth ewes from Walter Burrough and a further nine two teeth ewes from Rex Lovelace's dispersal sale. I borrowed an old stud ram to put with them, thus doing the whole job on a shoe-string.

The decision was vindicated five years later when I took three sheep to the Royal of England and returned with three first prizes, two cups, Breed Champion and Reserve Champion, opposite sex. The day the Dorsets were being judged, starting at nine-thirty, David and his wife, Sarah, were showing their Southdowns. Their judging started later, so it had been arranged that when the Dorsets were finished I would go and help them, as they had two strings of sheep out that day. But our plans went sadly wrong. After winning, I took my fellow competitors for the customary drink, which developed into two, or three, or four. Half way through this session someone reminded me that the Southdowns were out, but I was, by that time, in a state of blissful satisfaction. I could not have cared whether Southdowns or elephants were out – I had just won the Royal and was celebrating.

Eventually the party broke up and I made my way, somewhat unsteadily, back to the judging rings. All the Southdown classes had been judged and they were out for the championships. David had won with his pair of shearling ewes and Sarah with her shearling ram. I stood behind them on the rails to assess the situation; I was still just a little bit hazy. After a few minutes, though, it dawned on me that the championship rested between David's ewes and Sarah's ram. David was showing the ewes on his own and not making a very good job of it. Suddenly my mind cleared and I realised that I was supposed to be out there helping. I had visions of my daughter-in-law winning and, because I had not turned up to help as promised, I would be in for an earful from my son, most probably ably assisted by his mother. These thoughts sobered me up instantly. To get an ear bashing from either would be bad enough, but from both was to be avoided at all cost. Frank Grantham was judging and, waiting until he was busy at the bottom of the line with the ewe lambs, I slipped over the rails, walked up behind David and took one of the ewes from him. We straightened them up, showed them to perfection and won. I could breathe freely once again. Then we went back to the bar and celebrated a family double, during which the judge enquired: "Where the devil did you

spring from when we were judging the championships?'
Quite truthfully, I replied: "From up in the clouds."

After the house was renovated things began to fall into
place. More work came my way, much of which, being
trimming and shearing, was very seasonal, so I enlisted the
services of an old shepherding friend, George Payne, to
help me cut on occasions. He had retired from shepherding and is now a gardener. An ex-wartime Commando
Warrant Officer, he is very outspoken, with a great sense
of humour and has been very accurately described as "the
gentleman who swears". He is a great story-teller and is
always in demand at the local hunt's earth stoppers' sup-
pers. His standard depends entirely on his consumption of
whisky; half a bottle and he is quite respectable (not up to
Mothers' Union standards, but suitable for a wedding
reception). When his intake gets to the bottle mark the
level drops down to that of the earth stoppers' supper and
thereafter descends with great rapidity after each drink. I
have often thought that when we are working together,
two charges ought to be made – one for the work and
another for the entertainment!

Life had changed so much in a very short time. From living
in a town and coming home with nothing else to do but sit
and watch TV, I now have our own sheep to look after
before and after work and at weekends. It means more
work, but the pleasure gained is indescribable. And the great
joy is that once again we are living in the country.

The magic strikes me every time I return home. As I
turn off the A35 (coming from the east) on the top of the
high chalk ridge at Long Bredy Hut and drop down the
hill, the valley stretches out before me right down to the
sea at Burton Bradstock. Coming in from the west, again
off the A35, you descend Chalk Pit Hill and as you
bear sharp left half way down, the whole panorama of

the Bride valley stretches out before you. Apart from a few arable fields up under Puncknowle, the whole valley is a lush green, with the river gently flowing through the centre and its numerous tributaries meandering about before finally joining it. Litton Cheney nestles right under the steep escarpment of the downs, the beautiful church, with its magnificent fifteenth-century tower, standing like a sentinel on the high ground above the village. Across the valley, on the seaward slope, the villages of Puncknowle and Swyre almost join each other and, looking east up the valley, Long Bredy with Little Bredy and the source of the Bride are discernable in the distance. On turning that corner, I am always reminded of a line from "Jerusalem":

In England's green and pleasant land.

Besides the land we rent at Litton, we now have another nine acres about a mile to the west at Chilcombe, a tiny hamlet consisting of a farmhouse and a pair of cottages with the unique feature of a tiny Norman church right in the centre of the original farmyard. This extra land has enabled the flock to be increased and we now rear a dozen or so beef calves a year, selling them at about eight months old.

I have now joined that august band of old age pensioners and I sincerely hope that I shall spend the rest of my life here in the Bride valley. I may be a pensioner but I have not yet retired and have no intention of doing so until circumstances compel me to – and as mother used to say, "If you are a man, compel your circumstances." It is something I have endeavoured to do all my life, not always, I will admit, with success.

Many things have changed in my lifetime, not only in agriculture but also in the everyday life of so many people – great changes that have affected everyone and made life easier and more pleasant: electricity, piped water, radio, television and the ease and availability of transport, to name but a few. Regardless of what people say about the "good old days", everyone is really much better off today. This statement will, I have no doubt, raise some eyebrows, but when I think back to the days of my youth and remember the number of homeless tramps who used to walk from one workhouse to the next to get a bed for the night; of the old couples who had worked hard, long hours all their lives and when past work existed on a pension of a pound a week, then I give thanks that I was not of that generation.

As I sit writing this, at my grandfather's leather-topped desk in the front room of this lovely old house with its open fireplace and oak beams, with the pictures of dogs and sheep adorning the walls, I am acutely aware of how kindly Lady Luck has treated me for most of my life. My work has been my hobby as well as my livelihood. Through it I have had the honour to be presented to Her Majesty the Queen, the Duke of Edinburgh, the Prince of Wales and the Princess Royal and now, in the autumn of life, I can still continue doing what I love so dearly. It is said that farming is not so much a profession as a way of life – for me, sheep come into the same category.

This book is primarily about sheep and farming, so I have made little mention of my wife and family, but Dorothy has always supported me and has put up with my obsession with sheep for the last forty-four years. During all that time she has kept my feet firmly on the ground.

Russell, who made up his mind to be a carpenter while still at primary school, has followed in his grandfather's footsteps and now runs his own successful joinery and wheelwright business.

David, after an extremely successful career as a pedigree shepherd and showman, now farms with his wife on the

Isle of Wight. He has just been selected President-elect of the Southdown Sheep Society and will be President in 1994–5. Not only has he the honour of being elected to join those distinguished flock masters past and present, but, like the late John Craig and his son David (who is our present Chairman), we are among the very few in the one hundred-year history of the Society where both father and son have been President.

When looking back over life, the question sometimes passes through one's mind: if given the chance, would we do the same things again? As there is no likelihood of this happening, one tends to give an honest answer. Of course, with hindsight, one would not make the same mistakes again – and we have all made plenty of those!

But the two most momentous decisions that I made in life I would not alter. I would follow the same profession and I would marry the same girl.